# Playing for Rang

# PLAYING FOR RANGERS NO 15

## Edited by Ken Gallacher

## Stanley Paul
London Melbourne Sydney Auckland Johannesburg

Stanley Paul & Co. Ltd

An imprint of the Hutchinson Publishing Group

17–21 Conway Street, London W1P 6JD

Hutchinson Group (Australia) Pty Ltd
30–32 Cremorne Street, Richmond South, Victoria 3121
PO Box 151, Broadway, New South Wales 2007

Hutchinson Group (NZ) Ltd
32–34 View Road, PO Box 40–086, Glenfield, Auckland 10

Hutchinson Group (SA) (Pty) Ltd
PO Box 337, Bergvlei 2012, South Africa

First published 1983
© Stanley Paul & Co. Ltd 1983

Set in Linotron Baskerville by Input Typesetting Ltd

Printed in Great Britain by the Anchor Press Ltd
and bound by Wm Brendon & Son Ltd
both of Tiptree, Essex

ISBN 0 09 153681 2

Black and white photographs by courtesy of Sportapics
Colour photographs by Colorsport and Sportapics

*Frontispiece*: Jim Bett, seen here striding powerfully away from a tackle by West German star Pierre Littbarski. At the end of the season the Belgian side Lokeren paid a quarter of a million pounds to take him back there

# CONTENTS

# ANOTHER CHANCE - AND ALLY TAKES IT!

It became third time lucky for Rangers and the kid who had always supported them at the end of last season . . . .

For it was then that manager John Greig reaffirmed his search for success by buying Ally McCoist from Sunderland. The player cost Rangers just under £200,000 – but that was considerably less than he had cost the English First Division club two years earlier.

Rangers had tried for the twenty-year-old striker then, while he was still with St Johnstone. And before that they had tried to get him to Ibrox when he was a schoolboy.

This was the third time – and it worked out right for Rangers and for the player!

Said McCoist: 'I went to St Johnstone as a youngster because I knew there was more chance of getting first-team football there than there was at Ibrox.

'I was right then. I did get into the first team and I won Under-18 caps for Scotland and then several clubs came in to buy me.

'Rangers were one of them but then I decided on going to England simply because I thought it would make me a better player. I think that has worked out right for me too despite the fact that I have come home . . . .

'I believe I am a better player. The experience has helped me tremendously. OK, I was at a crossroads as far as my career was concerned but this move has made certain that I've taken the right turning.

'I supported Rangers as a kid and deep down I always wanted to play for them. This is my chance and I aim to take it.'

Greig, of course, had had to sustain the loss of midfield man Jim Bett and the probable non-return of Swedish star Robert Prytz. He moved quickly and before Celtic, Aberdeen or Dundee

Until last season this was how Ibrox fans knew Craig Paterson – as a centre half for Easter Road team Hibs

7

United could step in for the former St Johnstone man Greig had the deal fixed.

He admitted later: 'I had always admired Ally as a player and I knew that other people did as well. So I had to move quickly when the time came.

'I'm just delighted to add to the striking strength at Ibrox. Now we have three recognized strikers in Sandy Clark, John MacDonald and Ally. We need that.

'Also our style will suit Ally. We are a team who have to attack. We don't sit back and defend the way that Sunderland have to do for survival in the English First Division. That's not our way.

'We didn't get success last season by our own standards. Two Cup final appearances might satisfy some clubs . . . but not Rangers. So we have to do better and we have to have the players to make things happen. Ally McCoist can be one of them.'

The search continues, of course. Greig will not settle until he has a team which can claim the League title; the one honour he has not been able to take to Ibrox.

McCoist would like to help take that trophy there. He also relishes the thought of playing in Europe.

He says: 'As a youth player I loved to play in European matches. There was not much chance of doing that with Sunderland. Now here I am playing in the Cup Winners' Cup. It's all like a dream.'

A dream he hopes can come true. And one that will bring him the kind of success that Sunderland could never offer him.

The lure of Rangers remains powerful . . . .

# TO IBROX AT LAST
## by Sandy Clark

When Rangers' manager John Greig swooped swiftly into the transfer market last spring to sign Sandy Clark, it fulfilled a long-held ambition by the burly striker.

Clark had been signed by Airdrie when he was only thirteen years old and playing with a local school team. But his heart was always with Rangers. When he started making a reputation for himself as a goal scorer with the little Broomfield club, other top teams tried to buy him. Aberdeen were interested. Celtic came to try to buy him. But, always, Clark put off transfer talk hoping that the club he wanted to join most of all, Rangers, would come in for him.

At that time, though, Derek Johnstone was in scoring form at Ibrox and a striker was well down on the list of priorities. So Clark made a £200,000 move to West Ham. A little over six months later, when Derek Johnstone's scoring touch had deserted him, Greig moved, Clark returned from Upton Park and soon he was being tagged a latter day Colin Stein by the Ibrox faithful. Stein was a Rangers hero. Clark, at twenty-six years of age, wants to join him as a favourite of the fans.

Here in an interview with editor Ken Gallacher he talks about his career, his move to Ibrox and about his hopes for the future.

GALLACHER – It seems to have been a long way round for you . . . going south to the English First Division before finally finishing up exactly where you have always wanted to be.

CLARK – It was a kind of a roundabout way. But the most important thing as far as I'm concerned is that I have ended up at Ibrox. I enjoyed the little spell down at West Ham but when the chance came to come home and I was told that it was Rangers who wanted me, I didn't hesitate too long.

GALLACHER – Did you have any doubts at all in your mind about coming back north after just a short time in England?

CLARK – If I had been contemplating a move to some other club then there would have been doubts. But when the West Ham manager John Lyall spoke to me and said it was Rangers then that was different.

Right away I was 99 per cent certain that this was the one move I should make. That was without thinking it through properly.

GALLACHER – And now that you have had time to think it over – I mean after having a few months with the club and playing in one or two very important games – how do you feel now?

CLARK – I could never have made any better move. My immediate instincts were right. This is the club I had always wanted to play for. Honestly, I was happy at West Ham. I'd scored a few goals for them. I'd fitted in fine. The rest of the lads were good. There were a few Scots lads like Neil Orr and Raymond Stewart and they helped me settle in. But Rangers was something else again. Though I have to say I wouldn't have come home to any other club.

GALLACHER – Not even to Aberdeen who had wanted you earlier when you were still with Airdrie?

Sandy Clark, the Rangers striker, is on the ground here – but he got his shot in against St Mirren in the Scottish Cup semi-final replay at Hampden. Billy Thomson watches as it rises over the bar with full back Tom Wilson guarding the line just in case . . .

CLARK – No, not even to them. It was a good life down there in England. I mean, we stayed outside London so we didn't have the hassle of a big city. The other lads stayed close by and it wasn't much of a journey to the training ground each day. It was just the thought of playing at Ibrox which brought me back to Scotland. That and the prospect of playing in really important matches.

GALLACHER – Well you have done that already and you have some more to come don't you?

CLARK – Yes, that's the great thing about playing for a club such as Rangers. A few months with the club and I've played in the semi-final of the Scottish Cup and then the final. And we have qualified for Europe. Not forgetting the Old Firm games which are the biggest club games you can get. But Europe is an exciting prospect for me.

GALLACHER – Was that a factor in wanting to play for Rangers?

CLARK – Oh yes, that had to be a factor. I wanted to play for the club because I had supported them as a kid. That came first, a kind of emotional thing, if you like. But Rangers are almost always playing in Europe and that is something that even West Ham couldn't have guaranteed me. In fact there are only a few clubs down south who can say that they are in Europe every season. It's an event if Rangers don't make one of the three European competitions. Plus, of course, there was the thought of playing in a Cup final. Again, take a look at the Rangers record there – eight times at Hampden in succession. How many clubs can boast of that kind of Cup consistency? None apart from the club I've joined.

GALLACHER – Do you regret the fact that you didn't join Rangers straight from Airdrie?

CLARK – In the sense that I could have been here sooner – yes I do. But the time at West Ham wasn't wasted. I learned a great deal down there and it was a good place to go from that point of view.

GALLACHER – So the spell there wasn't time wasted?

CLARK – Most definitely not. John Lyall is one of the best coaches in the business. He works really hard with the players and I think that if you asked anyone in England you would find that he is one of the most respected managers in the game down there. The training was very good and it seemed light years ahead of anything I'd known up until then. Let's face it I'd been with Airdrie, a small part-time club and all we could do was train two or three nights a week. And even then, if the groundsman didn't want us on the playing field, that was that.

Striker Sandy Clark in the kind of action which reminds Rangers fans
of Colin Stein . . . dashing clear here from St Mirren defender John
McCormack in the Scottish Cup semi-final replay

You spent more time really keeping fit than you ever did working
on the skills of the game. You didn't have enough time to do
everything.

You finished work, went to the ground on training nights and
tried to make sure that your fitness was fine. Anything else was
hard to fit in. At West Ham – just as at Ibrox – time is taken
on different ball skills. You work hard on weaknesses you may
have in your game. You are given the chance to improve your
heading, say, or your running off the ball, or your shooting. Or
all of them at different times.

Down there at Upton Park they worked very, very hard on
touch play. Just one touch stuff. They wanted the ball played
up to me and for me to lay it off quickly and then move quickly
into position for a possible return. They were very hot on that
and I think I'm a better player because of the time I had there.
It may not have been long but the training was intensive. You
worked very hard and in that time, just those six or seven
months, I did more *real* training than in two or three seasons
with Airdrie.

GALLACHER – That was because of circumstances, though,
wasn't it? It wasn't that the Airdrie people didn't want to work
on your skills.

No messing about here by former Celtic star Johannes Edvaldsson
as he powers into a tackle against Sandy Clark in a Premier League
game against Motherwell at Ibrox

CLARK – Exactly. It was just that there wasn't enough time
to do all the things that the manager would have liked. I know
that Bobby Watson felt frustrated by this a lot of the time. He
was a great influence on me. He gave me good advice on and
off the field when he was boss at Broomfield. But being part
time just didn't allow you the opportunities that full-time players
get.

I really felt the difference when I went down to West Ham at
first and they were doing pre-season training. I'd always felt fit
enough but I was exhausted for the first few days.
GALLACHER – It must have been worth it to you, though, to
know that you would be competing on level terms.
CLARK – You're right. It was worth it. I think I realized in
that first week just what I'd been missing at Airdrie. I'm not

being critical of Airdrie because they were good to me for most of my time there. I didn't have too many complaints until near the end of my stay – and that was a dozen years remember. But to get the chance to be as fit as the men you are playing against is a great feeling. It was a bonus for me.

GALLACHER – I suppose that you have noticed this since coming back to Scotland, too?

CLARK – I probably notice it more because everything was so strange to me in England at first. I wasn't familiar with the different teams, the different players, the different systems. But coming back I'm in surroundings that I'm more used to. I can compare playing against other teams with Rangers, with what it was like when I was playing with Airdrie. I believe that has given me a better look at myself. I feel that I have improved in fitness and ability and I'll show that even more next season. The first few months at Ibrox I had a nagging groin strain. Not enough to stop me playing but painful enough to let me know that it was there most weeks. Then in the final I damaged my ligaments in the first half and had to play in the second half with a painkilling jag to help me through. It was enough to keep me in action but if there had been a replay I would have missed it. I could hardly walk the next day. That's OK now and the close season rest was what I needed for the groin strain. So I want to make my first full season something rather special for myself and the club.

GALLACHER – Some of the fans have compared you to Colin Stein who was such a favourite with the Rangers fans in the late sixties and the early seventies. Do you think there is any resemblance?

CLARK – I suppose there is in one way. I put myself about a bit and that is what he did as well. Also I like to try to give 110 per cent effort in every match. It's the way I've always played and it's the way I always will play. That is something that I think the fans like to see from players and I know that Steiny did that too. Maybe that's what they are thinking about. I hope that I can get as many goals for the club as he did.

GALLACHER – Would you set yourself any targets for goal scoring?

CLARK – I don't think so. As long as I can get my share. I'm just as happy if I can make space for someone else to get the goals – just as long as Rangers are winning games.

I managed to pick up one or two last season and unhappily there was controversy over two of the important ones. The first was at Tannadice against Dundee United and a lot of people gave that as an own goal. Well, it wasn't! That was important

to me because it got me off the mark, my first goal for Rangers and then there was doubt over it. I can assure you it was scored with a plain old-fashioned toe poke – not the kind Jimmy Hill talked about when Dave Narey scored against Brazil. This one was just a toe poke and nothing else. But like all the others it counted!

The other goal was even more controversial. It came in the replay against St Mirren at Hampden in the Scottish Cup semi-final. In the first game at Celtic Park we should have been runaway winners. If we had scored three or four goals it would have been about right. Yet somehow the game was criticized heavily. I didn't think it was all that bad. Semi-finals are no-toriously difficult games to play in. They are usually nervous, edgy games which produce few chances and not a lot of good football. The game was better than the critics thought.

The replay wasn't. It was a typical semi-final, both teams afraid of losing a goal. They were nervous, we were the same, because we all knew what was at stake – a place in the Hampden final against Aberdeen who had beaten Celtic in the other semi-final. Anyhow, towards the end of the match I scored and while the ball was cleared the referee gave the goal. He was right too. The ball was a good two feet over the line and the St Mirren keeper Billy Thomson admitted as much to me at the time. Later a few of the St Mirren players tried to say that the goal should have been disallowed. They didn't say that immediately after the incident. Billy was one I spoke to, others agreed with him. It was a goal and it took Rangers to the final. Their eighth in succession. My first ever!

GALLACHER – It wasn't one you could have enjoyed much, what with losing and being injured?

CLARK – You're right. I wanted so much to win a medal and then we lost in extra time. It was hard to take because beforehand everyone had written us off. We didn't believe the bookies, though. We felt we could do it and we did come close. There was no disgrace in the game, just disappointment!

GALLACHER – It was an astonishing sight to see the fans still cheering the team after the final whistle. So often they just seem to fade away from the terracings when the side loses.

CLARK – I'll never forget that. If anyone ever asks me why I

Who says the game is tougher in England? It doesn't seem that way to Sandy Clark as he returns from West Ham to meet up with Johannes Edvaldsson. Here he is sent sprawling in the Rangers v Motherwell clash

It was a bruising battle that day at Ibrox between Edvaldsson and Clark and here the Ibrox man is on top sending the big Icelandic defender the wrong way

wanted to join up at Ibrox then I think I'd just tell them to cast their minds back to that scene. They were magnificent.

GALLACHER – How have you found it settling in at Ibrox?

CLARK – It's been easy and I've been impressed with the set up. The training has been good but I know that it will be even better next year when I'm fully fit and when we don't have the midweek games always interrupting things. Tactically I have found that John Greig, the manager, and his assistant Tommy McLean, have been spot on in almost all the games we have played since I came into the side. And of course, there are good players to play alongside. Ally Dawson impressed me a lot.

When I left he was having a bad time because he had lost form after a nasty injury picked up in Canada while on tour with the club. But towards the end of the season, there he was back to his best and he deserved to be included in the Scotland squad for the home internationals and then taken on the three-match tour of Canada. He had come back to playing really well.

Young Dave McPherson was a revelation for me. I hadn't seen him before I went away and there he was suddenly in the first team and coping with everything so well, playing in top matches with not a sign of nerves. He was another player who deserved to be honoured by Scotland when they took him to Mexico for the world youth championships there.

GALLACHER – Are there other players who have impressed you?

CLARK – Quite a few of the younger boys around the place and especially watch out for Derek Ferguson. I saw him in a reserve game and he was like a man among boys – yet he is only sixteen years old himself. What a prospect he seems to be!

An Old Firm debut for Clark in the goalless draw at Celtic Park and here he battles it out for the ball with three Celts – midfield man Murdo Macleod, Paul McStay and defender Roy Aitken who attempts the vital clearance

GALLACHER – Any hopes for the future?
CLARK – The obvious ones. Helping Rangers win a trophy, scoring goals for the club and maybe having a wee run in Europe. That thought excites me as much as anything else.

Striker Sandy Clark who eventually reached his Ibrox goal after a transfer journey via West Ham

# JOY IN DORTMUND...

The long, long tradition of clashes between Rangers and the cream of West Germany's Bundesliga continued last season.

Down through the years the Ibrox side have battled with the best of the German sides in all three European tournaments – Borussia Moenchengladbach and Eintracht Frankfurt in the most prestigious of all, the European Cup; Bayern Munich, Borussia Dortmund and FC Cologne in the European Cup Winners' Cup and the Fairs Cup.

So when the draw was made for last year's UEFA Cup tournament, manager John Greig was scarcely surprised when Rangers were drawn with Borussia Dortmund in the first round.

As Greig pointed out: 'We have a fair working knowledge of West German football. We have played against them regularly in competition and we have undertaken tour games there over the years.

'They have a style which suits us to play against. We have come out evenly in our various battles. The games are always hard, always tactically difficult, but they are games we can look forward to playing in.'

Rangers had played themselves into a European frame of mind gradually with their pre-season trip to France. And they were given a further pointer to the strengths of Borussia when Celtic played them in a pre-season match in West Germany and won.

Greig wisely did not go to watch them in that match realizing that the Germans would be under strength. But he did see them later and his respect for them grew.

They had Rumanian World Cup star Marcel Radacanu controlling play in midfield, and up front the powerful striker Manfred Burgsmuller was being hailed as successor to Horst Hrubesch for international recognition. There were others, too, with formidable reputations. More than that Borussia, out to recapture old glories, had forced themselves to the top of the Bundesliga in that early part of the season.

The first match was away from home in the magnificent

The sight that the defenders of Borussia Dortmund learned to hate in the second leg of their UEFA Cup game at Ibrox . . . Davie Cooper, the Ibrox match-winner, leaving an opponent struggling

stadium built in the industrial city of Dortmund for the 1974 World Cup. Scotland had opened their campaign there that time around and now it was Rangers' turn. Their aim was a long run in Europe – but the determined Dortmund side wanted the same. For too many years they had been languishing in the shadows of a new generation of Germans. Bayern, Fortuna Dusseldorf, their namesakes of Moenchengladbach and Hamburg had all overtaken them since the great days when they had boasted several of West Germany's 1966 World Cup squad and had beaten Liverpool in a Hampden final of the Cup Winners' Cup.

The names of Sigi Held and Lothar Emmerich were fading memories to the new supporters who wanted to see their team reach for glory once more.

Greig realized that he was up against a team who wanted to prove themselves a power in the land again. He knew, too, that his own re-cast team was still settling into the kind of modern, studied play he wanted from them.

Two of the new signings Dave McKinnon and Craig Paterson had not played in competitive European football before.

As Greig pointed out: 'There is a fair bit of pressure on any player who has not been in a European tie before. That's natural.

'And it's not as if they are getting a nice, comfortable easy tie to settle themselves down. They are not. We are facing a team who are in second place in the Bundesliga, arguably one of the hardest leagues in the world. I'm confident enough in their ability but there is no way you can be over-confident when it's this calibre of opposition you have to face.'

Greig had decided early on that the key to success against the West German side would be the performance of his newly un-veiled central defensive partnership of Northern Ireland inter-national John McClelland and the £200,000 buy from Hibs, Craig Paterson.

McClelland had returned as a star after his performances for the Irish in Spain. They had done superbly in the World Cup finals, reaching the second stage and winning the hearts of the fans back home in Britain. And McClelland had become a local hero to Rangers supporters from Northern Ireland who had their own little fan club for him in Madrid!

Meanwhile the lean and powerful Paterson had settled in alongside the Irishman, forming a defensive double act which was quickly establishing itself.

The other new face to Europe was full back Dave McKinnon, a surprise buy from Partick Thistle in the close season. A bar-gain at less than £30,000, the red-haired McKinnon was soon being compared to that old Ibrox warhorse Bobby Shearer be-cause of the power and tenacity of his tackling.

It was hard to believe that he had fought back from a cruel illness which had come close to threatening his career. Just two years earlier McKinnon had a damaged kidney removed – now here he was ready to play in Europe.

'All I want is to do my best for Rangers,' said McKinnon, 'because they have given me the chance of a lifetime. It's still hard to believe that I'm preparing for Europe instead of playing as a part-timer with Partick Thistle. I feel so fit, now, with the

It's that man Cooper again, in the form which saw him score once and make another for striker Derek Johnstone in the UEFA Cup game with Borussia Dortmund

training I have had here. No one can have any doubts left about that.'

No one did. And McKinnon did make his debut in Europe against the high flying Germans.

The game was a fifty-four thousand sell out in the marvellous stadium, giving the German team a quarter of a million pounds gate bonanza. It also produced problems for manager John Greig as he continued the fight to keep trouble from the terracings when Rangers fans went abroad.

As Greig explained, it is an easy enough matter to restrict ticket sales in Glasgow and run checks on all those who are travelling. So often on the Continent the problem can come from the Forces stationed in West Germany. Two Scottish regiments were based in and around Dortmund and Greig made a special visit to speak to all the men who were attending the game. Two thousand listened to him and respected the message, and of the four thousand fans who went to support the team no one was in trouble.

Midfield man Jim Bett, one of the architects of the Rangers result against Dortmund, carries the ball clear of a tackle from one of the West German defenders

That important off-field performance was matched on the field by the commitment and tactical know-how of the Ibrox side. Before the game Greig had emphasized that they could not afford to slip up as they had in their dismal defeat in Prague a year earlier against Dukla.

A moment's relaxation on a night of lashing rain had given the Czechs an early goal, boosted their confidence and eventually sent Rangers slithering to defeat.

Still, there was a more formidable look to the team since those days. McClelland and Paterson were in and looking good, Robert Prytz, the close-season buy from Sweden, was linking well with Jim Bett in the midfield and Dave McKinnon had been a revelation.

But all of them knew that this was to be their biggest test so far. . . .

Yet, when it came, Rangers passed with flying colours. This was one of their best nights on the Continent, bringing back memories of their blood and guts struggle against the same team fifteen years earlier. They were underdogs then, playing the Cup Winners' Cup holders. And in that far off time before substitutes were allowed, they played for a large part of the game with only ten men. At the end the scoreline was 0-0 and Rangers went through.

This time, at the end of the first leg, the giant scoreboard in the stadium flashed the same score to the capacity crowd. And beneath its glow the Rangers players took a victory salute in front of their own group of supporters.

It was a memorable opening night in Europe for a new-look team. Yet it could have been even better. In the first half, Derek Johnstone, only recently recalled to the side after injury, hit the bar with a powerful drive. And late in the game he watched helplessly as one of the West German defenders cleared another brilliant header off the goal line with the keeper beaten.

Sure, Rangers had anxious moments themselves to survive. In the first fifteen minutes, though, they stood firm against the desperate Dortmund attacks. They weathered that storm and then they settled down to play a kind of possession football which gave Borussia problems they could not handle. Jim Bett was the general who dictated play in one of his finest games for the Ibrox club.

But it was a night when all of the players contributed something . . . a night when their rewards could have been greater, but were still enough to give them hope for an Ibrox victory which would carry them into the next round of the tournament.

The omens continued to look right as the build up to the second leg in two weeks' time began to take shape.

Rangers' impressive start to the season continued. For the first time in eight years the Ibrox team travelled north to Pittodrie and returned with a Premier League win. Only Derek Johnstone had been playing the last time Rangers recorded a league victory there. This time he scored one of the goals while Robert Prytz got the other. That came just four days before the Dortmund return – and their news was far from good. They lost 3-2 away from home to Nuremberg and also lost their giant defender Rolf Russmann with a broken arm. He was the man they wanted to deal with the aerial power of Johnstone . . . and now he was out and a reserve would have to be drafted in.

There were scares, too, for the Scots when Dave McKinnon, Craig Paterson and Johnstone all missed the Monday training session. However all joined the player pool which travelled down the Ayrshire coast to Troon to get in shape for the European second leg tie.

One of the few anxious moments for Rangers in the second-leg game against Borussia. Jim Stewart has saved at the feet of the West German skipper Manfred Burgsmuller who goes down as John McClelland and Ally Dawson look on worriedly

The worry for manager Greig wasn't so much the injuries, but the problems which come with a 0-0 result away from home. The fans look on that as a victory . . . managers realize that to lose a goal places you under pressure. For away goals in European tournaments count double and a Dortmund draw would take them through instead of Rangers.

Greig also realized that the well-organized Germans would make things very hard for Rangers.

He pointed out: 'We must show discipline here. There is no use being urged on by the fans and then forgetting that we must keep the door shut at the back. You can't simply charge forward looking for goals. What we have to aim for is playing all our football in their half of the field, trying to put them under pressure as much as possible, but always making sure that we are not vulnerable to the quick breaks that German teams are so good at. The fans must be patient too. They can help us a lot by not demanding too much too early.'

On the night Ibrox was a near sell out. Forty-four thousand fans brought the new-look stadium to life and Greig made just one change from the first leg, bringing in young John MacDonald up front instead of midfielder Ian Redford.

The fans roared on their team, but as Greig had forecast, patience was necessary. The West Germans were methodical in their defence and inspired in their breaks which were prompted mainly by the talented Rumanian Radacanu. Twice in a nervous opening spell the Rangers defence was caught out and twice Jim Stewart was swift enough to stop the Germans scoring.

It was no more than Rangers had expected. Soon after that opening flurry the Germans sat back and Rangers began to push forward in numbers. Jim Bett, Ally Dawson, Robert Prytz and Davie Cooper all came close to breaking the deadlock in a first half which was dominated intelligently by the Scots. There were

It was performances similar to the one he gave against Borussia which earned Jim Bett the Scotland jersey he is seen wearing here

none of the old-fashioned cavalry raid charges so beloved of the old Rangers teams. Instead there was a disciplined and orderly build up designed to find gaps in the Dortmund defence and to find space against a team dedicated to denying them.

And so, it was almost on the stroke of half time when the Rangers players gave their huge support the goal they wanted so much. Prytz crossed, Johnstone rose majestically to head the ball down into the goal area and, after a shot from Robert Russell was blocked, Davie Cooper moved in for the kill. He hit the ball over the line and with the German defence in tatters Rangers had pushed themselves towards the second round of the UEFA Cup tournament.

Of course the game was not over, but Rangers were in control by this time. They had more chances and missed them. They had fine midfield play, good passing movements and scarcely a second of danger from the Germans.

The second goal took longer to arrive than expected, but when it did come it proved all the earlier West German fears correct. They had worried over Johnstone's heading power, and worried over the loss of Russmann. The first goal had suggested the weakness was there – the second confirmed it. Cooper crossed from the right and there was the burly striker rising above everyone and ramming a header in at the far post. A classic Rangers goal and one which sent the fans home dreaming of the next round and wondering which of the top teams in Europe would be visiting Ibrox in the near future. . . .

Would the draw bring them Benfica of Portugal, or Anderlecht of Belgium, one of the teams from behind the Iron Curtain, or perhaps, for a change, an easier passage to the next round with a game against the small fry from the Scandinavian countries.

A few days later the draw was made and once more Rangers found themselves heading for Germany. The coincidence which has thrown so many Rangers sides into action against the Germans had struck again. Time after time they have been drawn with a Bundesliga team while their greatest rivals, Celtic, have yet to play in Germany in a competitive European game!

They were drawn against old rivals, FC Cologne, who they had beaten once before in the old Fairs Cities Cup, the forerunner of the tournament they were now playing in. And a few years earlier, under Greig's management, they had lost to them in the quarter-finals of the European Cup.

Old scores had to be settled but as the fans dreamed of further European glory they could not know that they were heading into a nightmare. . . .

# ...AND DISASTER IN COLOGNE!

This was the third time I had travelled with Rangers to meet the West Germans from Cologne.

In 1968 in the old Fairs Cities Cup, they won 4-3 on aggregate before finally going out of the competition to the eventual winners, Leeds United, in the quarter-finals.

It had been tough then but it had come at a bad time, just as manager Scot Symon had been sacked, coach Bobby Seith resigned and Davie White appointed manager. The home leg was won 3-0 but, as always in Cologne, a fiery second leg found Rangers battling to hold on. They did – but only just as they crashed 3-1 in that second leg.

The second time, in the Mungersdorf Stadium, Rangers went down 1-0 to a goal from international striker Dieter Muller. That was in John Greig's first year as manager and the new boss had guided the side to stunning victories over the Italian champions Juventus and then the Dutch kings, PSV Eindhoven, in the opening rounds of the European Cup.

Cologne came next in the quarter-final and after losing just 1-0 away from home it looked as if Rangers would reach the last four of Europe's top tournament. But it was not to be. Another goal from Dieter Muller put Rangers behind in the second leg at Ibrox and while a Tommy McLean free kick near the end salvaged some of the Scots' pride, Cologne had gained revenge for that defeat eleven seasons earlier.

Now the paths of the two teams crossed again – and Cologne looked even more formidable rivals to Rangers' European dreams than Dortmund had been in the first round. They were behind Borussia in the Bundesliga, but ahead of them on personality players – and on a personality coach. For bossing the Cologne team was Rinus Michels, once in charge of Ajax of Amsterdam and the Dutch international team and Barcelona too.

Now the soccer mercenary had joined Cologne boosting his huge bank balance by several million marks and trying to guide them back to the glories they had once known.

The West German coach Rinus Michels called it a battle at Ibrox
when Cologne met Rangers there in the second round of the UEFA
Cup . . . but who started the fighting:
Young John MacDonald is jostled by the West German Under-21
midfield ace Stefan Engels
MacDonald tries to recover only to be hurled to the ground by
Engels with the ball nowhere near the players

It looked as if the tie was coming at the right time for Rangers. Their early form had continued to impress. The settling down process for the new boys, started in France, had continued in the League Cup and in the opening League matches and the European tie against Dortmund.

Yet they had worries, as well. Craig Paterson was the victim of a recurring injury and the influential Jim Bett was hurt in the 2-2 draw with St Mirren at Love Street as they limbered up for their second assault on Europe.

It was significant that the Saints boss Ricky McFarlane went out of his way to praise the new style Rangers after that game. 'All my players came into the dressing room talking about how changed Rangers were,' commented McFarlane. 'We enjoyed the game because Rangers were concentrating completely on playing good, flowing, entertaining football.

'It's the kind of football which brings success in Europe and as far as I'm concerned I'd say that they are really well equipped for European football now.'

It was an unsolicited tribute from a fellow professional and it gave an added boost to the prospects of the Scots. Yet Greig knew that all the tributes in the world would not help unless his team hit the form they had shown in the previous round.

This time there is no recovery as he is sent crashing from behind while West German skipper Gerd Strack ignores the off-the-ball clash

Cologne had four players in their team who had been in the West German team which beat England 2-1 at Wembley in the previous week. They were the World Cup villain, goalkeeper Harald Schumacher, sweeper Gerd Strack and forwards Pierre Littbarski and Klaus Allofs. Another of their stars, Stefan Engels had played for the Under-21 team against England, while, besides the current internationals, they also had World Cup striker Klaus Fischer who had now retired from the national side. Fischer was injured, but a rather well-known deputy stood by if he failed to make it. His name was Rainer Bonhof who had gone back home to West Germany after a successful stay in Spain with Valencia.

This, then, was the calibre of the opposition!

As Greig stressed: 'The win at Wembley will have given their four players a tremendous boost. And look at what Littbarski did, played in Germany in the Under-21 game and then came on as a substitute at Wembley. He scored a hat trick in the first match and made two goals in the second. That is some going. . . .

'They will be walking tall because a win at Wembley does that for any Continental team. It certainly doesn't make things any easier for us.'

MacDonald is flattened and Engels moves away from the scene of the crime!

The 'battle' continues – and Rangers are still on the receiving end.
Cologne skipper Strack catches Jim Bett late as the Ibrox man takes
the ball past him

But when the West Germans arrived they did so cautiously.
Littbarski, his country's idol after that international double
header the previous week, admitted that he was back to his best
form.

But then he added: 'I'd say I was happy with the way I
played last week. But we always have to remember that in
Britain the strength of the game lies with the club sides. We
always find it easier to play against your international teams
than we do against your clubs.

'I don't know why this is. But there is no doubt that all of the
players in Germany believe that to be the case. If we have a
choice in these matters then we would always want to avoid
your British teams in club competitions but we would not worry
so much if we met them internationally.

'There is a great difference. Perhaps it is because we place
more emphasis on the national team. Your clubs here always
appear to come first in priority.

'Still, my form is back and until the games last week it had been a problem for me. Now I want to keep it and perhaps if we can hold Rangers to a single goal lead we will be able to go through.

'It will be very, very hard for us even to get a draw and we cannot afford to lose a goal early in the game. We know about Rangers from the Dortmund match – this is a difficult match for us to face.'

It was just as much of a problem for Rangers. At Troon where the team were preparing for the game Greig admitted: 'I am more worried over this game than I was over the one against Borussia Dortmund. I recognized Borussia as a hard-working and well-organized team. They showed all the qualities of efficiency we have come to expect from the West Germans. But all along I've felt that Cologne will have more flair than them. They have more players who are capable of turning a game on their own. This is an added worry.

'All I want to do is win the game – that is the aim. I'm not putting any scoring targets in front of my players. But I do want to avoid losing a goal to them here at Ibrox. Away goals could be important if the tie is as tight as we all expect.'

Thirty-two thousand fans were at Ibrox for the match and they saw Derek Johnstone step from the shadows to give his team the lead after only nine minutes. It was the start Rangers had wanted . . . the start that Cologne and their stars had dreaded.

It all happened so easily too. A throw in from Swedish star Robert Prytz found Davie Cooper. As the ball reached him he hit an overhead kick into the Cologne penalty box and with the Germans caught out Johnstone moved onto the ball and hooked a vicious shot out of the reach of Schumacher.

That put Rangers in command and it was twenty-six long minutes before Jim Stewart, in the Rangers goal, had a single shot to hold. Even then it was a low, trundling, long-range try from Cologne's Yugoslav midfielder Ednem Slijvo.

Meanwhile Paterson had watched a header cleared from the line by Harald Konopka, Schumacher had strung together a series of saves and Robert Prytz had missed an open goal from a dozen yards range. At half time it seemed only a matter of how many goals Rangers might be able to add. Indeed, if all the chances had gone in, the return in the cathedral town of Cologne would have been a formality.

How wrong all these thoughts were to prove. . . .

With things going badly the Germans began to mix it to the fury of the Rangers fans. Slijvo was booked for a foul on Jim

Bett and Gerd Strack for a wild tackle on Cooper. These came in the opening few minutes of the second half and the tactics were clearly designed to anger and upset the Scots. These, plus a hotly disputed equaliser in the sixtieth minute, did exactly that.

The goal came from nothing. A free kick was given after a powerful tackle by John McClelland on Stefan Engels. The tricky little Littbarski took it and played it to Klaus Allofs who scored with a drive which Jim Stewart could only help into the net. But angry Rangers players surrounded Swedish referee Rolf Ericsson. Their claim – later supported by television evidence – was that Littbarski had played the ball twice before Allofs touched it. That is a breach of the rules and yet the Germans survived the appeals which were waved aside. The goal stood and suddenly Rangers were in trouble.

They could have, and should have, had a penalty after that when Prytz was flattened in the box but it was not their night.

Frustration set in and Derek Johnstone and Ian Redford were both booked. Then Craig Paterson was carried off after a nasty

This time Harald Konopka is floored after an incident with John MacDonald

tackle from behind by Allofs. In the end Rangers did go in front for the second leg. With five minutes to go Davie Cooper, maker of the first goal, stepped in once more to set up a chance. It was with a beautifully placed free kick which this time McClelland headed into the net past the helpless Schumacher.

The problem was whether it would be enough, and the general concensus was that Rangers were going to face the fight of their lives to hang onto that lead in West Germany in the return match.

It was still easy to remember how much they had dominated the game . . . how often they had had chances to score . . . how badly dealt with they were by the referee over that so controversial equaliser.

Yet it was also easy to remember how hard it is for any team to hold onto a single goal lead against a team of proven ability. Cologne were such a team and when Rangers lost to Celtic at Celtic Park, after holding a 2-1 lead, just a few days before the return, things looked bleak.

The West Germans don't like it and MacDonald is threatened as the Swedish linesman pushes Gerd Strack away from the young Ibrox forward

They liked this even less as Harald Schumacher is beaten by a shot from Derek Johnstone (not in the picture) for the first goal. Jim Bett who had followed up turns away in delight

But while Rangers had lost to their greatest rivals only in the closing minutes, Cologne fared even more badly. They had brought back the injured Klaus Fischer and had still gone down to Eintracht Frankfurt by 3-0. It was the shock result of the Bundesliga.

Rangers, however, had more to worry them than simply the match itself. A campaign had been stirred up by the West Germans against the Scots. Rinus Michels had begun it after the first game when he talked of 'rough play' from Rangers. The West German press continued the smear campaign even though in the first game Cologne had started the trouble.

These reports concerned Rangers so much that they brought them to the attention of the European Union, the Continent's soccer bosses. They made no protest but they pointed out that the allegations made against the team did not in any way find support in either the official UEFA observer's report or the report from the referee.

They were right to be worried. Twenty years earlier I had been in Cologne when the same type of hate campaign had been whipped up against Dundee. And the outcome was trouble – big trouble!

Dundee had gone there leading by an amazing 8-1 score from the first leg of the European Cup tie at Dens Park. But the German fury was directed at an injury sustained by their veteran keeper Fritz Ewert early in the game after a collision with centre forward Alan Cousin. They left Scotland vowing vengeance – and they took their vengeance in the return match.

When goalkeeper Bert Slater took his place in goal a first-aid team with a stretcher sat down immediately beside the goal posts. Slater told me later: 'They made it plain from the start that the stretcher was there for me. They wanted me off.'

That's the way that game went. Slater was carried off with concussion after only twenty-six minutes and Andy Penman, later to join Rangers, had to take over in goal until the keeper recovered in the second half.

At the end only the intervention of Scots' troops stationed at Minden helped the Dundee players escape from a mob which invaded the pitch. Cologne won that game 4-0 and missed a penalty.

The omens did not look good and they appeared worse on the night before the match. Just twenty minutes after starting their scheduled one hour work out under the lights at the Mungersdorf Stadium the ground was plunged into darkness.

Rangers were left to finish off their preparations in the shadowy light of the street lamps on a piece of waste ground outside the stadium. Under European Union rules every team is entitled to that one hour session on their opponent's ground.

Said an angry Greig: 'All we have been told is that the lights failed. That's all. Not another word. Not even an apology.'

The Scots were clearly bitter at the latest incident but Greig refused to be drawn into any slanging match. 'We are here to play football,' he stressed, 'not become involved in any off-field rows designed to upset people and to sell tickets. We want to win and we honestly believe we can do so despite all the hassle we have had to put up with. It's not a very nice situation but there are times when you have to deal with this kind of thing in Europe. It has happened to us before and no doubt it will happen again. We have to try to make sure that we concentrate totally on the job in hand.'

That was what Greig hoped to do. It was what he hoped his players would be able to do. But, in front of a huge crowd of sixty-one thousand people, fourteen minutes wrecked all the carefully laid plans that had been made by the men from Ibrox. Fourteen minutes which must rank among the worst minutes ever suffered by a Rangers team in any game, in any country.

Fourteen minutes which saw the team most people believed

to be the most promising seen at Ibrox in many seasons humbled, humiliated and destroyed. . . .

Fourteen minutes which were to scar an entire season. For there is no doubt that these crucial minutes left their mark on the players until the season was almost over. It took a long, long time for Rangers to recover from the blitzkrieg which was fired by the artistry of little Pierre Littbarski.

It was the tiny wing wizard who started the troubles which brought Rangers disaster. After only seven minutes he wriggled his way past two bemused Rangers defenders and then found space to play a one-two with Klaus Allofs and strike the return pass beyond Jim Stewart and into the net off the inside of the far post.

Just minutes before that Derek Johnstone had dropped a header onto the roof of the net and, even though they were without injury victim Craig Paterson, Rangers had started confidently enough. After the goal they fell apart. . . .

In eleven minutes Klaus Fischer drove a cross deep to the far post where Stefan Engels met it and volleyed in a shot which hit the underside of the bar and crossed the line. . . .

In nineteen minutes another cross, from Allofs this time, beat the Rangers defence. Littbarski headed the ball for goal, Jim Stewart pushed it out but Fischer followed it up and forced the ball over the line. . . .

In twenty-one minutes Engels went down in a tackle with Dave McKinnon. Karoly Palotai, the Hungarian referee, gave a penalty and Engels scored from the spot.

It was all over!

The game had been won and lost in that seemingly short space of time. Short and swift for the West German executioners – but surely the longest night in memory for the stunned Rangers players and fans.

The final acts of the tragedy had not been played out. Harald Schumacher brought back memories of the summer in Spain with a wild tackle on Jim Bett which should have brought Rangers a second half penalty. It equalled his vicious World Cup foul – but play was waved on and Bett was left with vivid scars as a souvenir of his meeting with the West German keeper.

Seven minutes into the second half Allofs scored a fifth and while Willmer was ordered off late in the game nothing could ease the Rangers hurt.

And this made it still worse – Schumacher fails to get to a cross and Rangers skipper John McClelland heads the ball into the net for the second goal. This was the one which won the first leg at Ibrox

It was the worst defeat I have witnessed and I have been following them in Europe for seventeen long years. It remains, also, the most mystifying.

How was it possible for a team to collapse so dramatically against a side they had outplayed and outclassed just two weeks earlier?

How could the absence of just one player, centre half Craig Paterson, make such a difference to a defence which had looked solid and reliable in so many other games?

How could a team which had shown discipline and tactical know-how against Borussia Dortmund become little boys lost against a team which ranked behind Dortmund in the League?

These were questions no one could answer. Questions which were being asked of each other by bewildered Rangers fans as they sat disconsolately in the beer halls of Cologne contemplating another failure in Europe.

They were being asked the next day, too, by the players and manager John Greig. Even they could not explain just where things had gone wrong. They did not seek excuses in the hate campaign which had undoubtedly turned the game into an ordeal for them before a ball had been kicked.

Team boss John Greig, as shell-shocked as anyone told me: 'I took a look at that giant scoreboard and I simply could not believe my eyes. I had gone into the game genuinely believing that we could reach the next round of the tournament. Then, there we were out in such a short time. The players didn't deserve that. There was never that kind of gap between the sides. It just seemed in that spell that anything Cologne did was going to end up in the net. Two of the goals went in off the woodwork, another came after a save by Jim Stewart . . . it was one of those nights for them.

'I remember playing for Rangers against Real Madrid and they hit six goals past us in the Bernabeu Stadium. That was hard to take at the time, but I think we all knew that night that we had been outclassed. This time we weren't so very far behind the Germans. We should have won much more convincingly than we did in the first leg at Ibrox.

'If the same game was to be played next week then I would stand by the same team and the same tactics. I felt sorry for the supporters because this is one of the few times when they have left a foreign ground without being able to hold their heads high. I really do feel for them.'

And so the team which had promised so much had crashed – and the full extent of the crash was still to be discovered.

# INTO THE BIG TIME– ALMOST!
## by Craig Paterson

The season which ended last summer, my first as a Rangers player, should have been the most memorable of my whole career to date.

And it was – but in two wildly different ways. One, because for the first time as a senior player I took part in two Cup finals and also made the break into European football.

And two, because what should have been the highspot of my soccer life was turned into a near nightmare by a nagging injury which I picked up early in the season.

Last season's big money buy, centre half Craig Paterson moving into action during one of his early games for Rangers

So instead of being able to help Rangers through the bad spell they had in mid-season, I spent most of the time on the treatment table. It's the worst year I have ever known for injuries. In the two previous seasons when I was playing with Hibs I missed just one match. It was a mid-week game, a rearranged fixture against Dundee at Dens Park and I was out because I was on international duty with the Scotland Under-21 team!

Not a single injury in two years and then out for weeks and weeks on end. It turned the season into one of frustration for me. Yet, at the same time, there is no denying that I was given glimpses of the greatness which can be achieved by Rangers and the club's players.

It was for that I made the move from Hibs. I had spent a long time there and my father had played with them before me. But, in the end, I was glad to make the change and even more glad to be getting the chance to join Rangers.

I've always been ambitious and with Hibs while I was there the main ambition seemed to be to try to stay in the Premier League. So when we went out to play matches the manager Bertie Auld's constant maxim was 'Don't lose a goal – and that means you won't lose the game!' There was rarely any talk of going out to win games and that had a dulling effect on players. You didn't want to try too much. If you did try something and you lost the ball then you were going to be in bother with the Boss. It was as simple as that. Someone playing centre forward was liable to be substituted if he wasn't closing down the central defenders. Never mind scoring – just stop them playing. That was the code. It didn't suit me and I think I showed that in my first half-dozen games with Rangers. I scored four times then, revelling in the freedom I was getting. That was more than I scored in the two seasons before that.

Unhappily the injury came along and my goal scoring exploits came to an end. But the point I am making is that defenders at Ibrox are given freedom to go forward if there is a move on. That didn't happen with Hibs and it doesn't happen with too many of the teams in the Premier League where survival is the major consideration.

Still, while I missed so much of the season I did get involved enough to realize the gulf which exists between playing for a

A tussle here between two former members of Scotland's successful Under-21 team . . . striker Frank McAvennie of St Mirren tries to get the better of the powerful Rangers centre half Craig Paterson

provincial side such as Hibs and with a top club like Rangers. Take the start of the season. I had just had one day's training with Hibs when my transfer to Rangers took place. The next day I was on a plane for France and a pre-season tournament there. Forty-eight hours later I was facing St Etienne and some of the stars of that exciting French World Cup squad. Then I followed up with a game against Lokeren of Belgium and some of their World Cup men. . . .

Now, if I'd stayed with Hibs the pre-season preparations would have been a whole lot different. It would have been a bus journey north into the Highlands and three matches there against Highland League opposition. Games, I think, against Ross County, Inverness Caley and Keith. Not too much glamour attached to that little jaunt is there?

Not just that, of course, but while it does help you tune up for the season which is going to follow, it doesn't teach you too much about the game. There isn't a lot you can pick up from playing against Highland League teams. I'm not being disrespectful at all. It's just a simple fact of life that when you play top teams from Europe there is always something fresh you can come up against and that is when you can make most improvement in your play.

Up front helping the attack as he likes to do, Craig Paterson in the background watches as Cologne defender Harald Konopka heads a try from Derek Johnstone off the line in the UEFA Cup first-round game at Ibrox

At least I did get a brief taste of Europe last season – and I know that is only a beginning. I hope that this year we can push through further in the Cup Winners' Cup tournament.

Anyhow, I did enjoy the games against the two West German teams Borussia Dortmund and Cologne, even though these were the games which brought me the injury.

First of all against Dortmund a player fell on my ankle and that started off the trouble . . . but in the next round against Cologne I was the victim of a vicious tackle from behind.

I'm not certain still whether it was Klaus Allofs or Stefan Engels who brought me down. All I do know is that the tackle was late. I had played the ball when the German player came in and whacked me. It was the same ankle and that was the start of a season's misery for me.

From then on it was a battle all the time to try to get back to fitness. In a way it was my own fault that I could not relax and try to allow time to work its own cure. There were too many important games around that time and so I pushed myself to try to play in them all. We had been going so well, the team was looking good, my own form had been fine, and I had been tasting the kind of atmosphere that had been missing in so many of the matches we played with Hibs.

Ibrox star Craig Paterson rates Celtic's Frank McGarvey as one of his toughest opponents. It's easy to see why he thinks that way when you look at this New Year's Day clash between the two of them. McGarvey tries to push the big Rangers defender off the ball

So instead of listening to advice from the backroom staff I kept forcing the issue. I wanted to play in the first Old Firm game of the season . . . I wanted to play in the return game in Cologne . . . I wanted to play in the League Cup clashes with Hearts . . . I wanted to play in the League Cup final.

I made that one and we lost and the injury played me up again afterwards. It was a hard decision for me to make and harder for me to accept from others that rest was the only answer. But that's the way it turned out.

I'm sure that I'll know better if it ever happens to me again – though I'm praying that injuries are behind me now. I think I've suffered enough in my first season to last me right through my Ibrox career!

If it had not been my first season then perhaps I would have been able to sit back, look at things logically and calmly and wait for the treatment to work. But, because it was my first season I was desperate to get back into action. After all, these games I mentioned were all *big* games. They were what I wanted most when I made the move in the summer. That was what playing for Rangers meant and I didn't want to let them down. The club had given me my chance, the supporters had given me a tremendous welcome, and I felt that I had to repay that.

I still feel that way. Believe me I'll give everything I have got to help bring Rangers success!

The success we want is victory in the Premier League. Make no mistake about that. We want it for the fans more than anything else. It is the hardest honour to win because the Premier League must be as competitive a league as any in Europe.

I found in the matches I played against Continental opposition last season that defenders get far more time on the ball than they ever do in domestic games. I'm talking about the two pre-season matches and the three games I had against the top German teams. Now the West German league is supposed to be a hard one to play in and I don't doubt that. They have some tremendous players and their tactics and technique keep proving themselves in club and international football. But even against them, I found that I could find time to control the ball and then time, too, to move forward. They seem ready to lie off you a little, pulling back to restrict space for the attacking players in the opposing side. In Scotland it isn't like that at all. When you get the ball you find an opponent coming in to challenge you as

*Opposite*: Eye on the ball and John MacDonald moves into a familiar role, leaving a trail of defenders in his wake

*Above*: Right on the ball . . .
Rangers full back Ally Dawson
powers his way to win a
challenge leaving Aberdeen
winger Peter Weir flat out

*Right*: Up and away . . . as
Rangers centre half Craig
Paterson outjumps Aberdeen
striker Eric Black in the Cup
final

*Opposite above*: Waiting for
the off . . . the Rangers team,
plus substitutes, are joined by
manager John Greig as they
line-up for the official
presentations before the
Scottish Cup final

*Opposite below*: Double
defence as Peter McCloy and
Dave McPherson make sure a
Ranger gets to the ball in the
Cup final

*Above*: Dave MacKinnon, who made a considerable impact at full back and in midfield in his first Ibrox season, shows his determination to beat off a St Mirren challenge

*Opposite above left*: All the sevens . . . Davie Cooper of Rangers takes on Aberdeen's Gordon Strachan

*Opposite above right*: Rangers captain John McClelland keeps an eye on events in the Scottish Cup final

*Opposite below*: The perfect strike . . . as Robert Russell of Rangers beats a St Mirren defender to get in his shot during a game at Ibrox

*Opposite*: New signing Sandy Clark shows the power and purpose that made Rangers swoop to sign him from West Ham

*Right*: Heads . . . and Ally Dawson wins this duel in the air against a St Mirren opponent

*Below:* Attack v defence . . . as Rangers front men take on the St Mirren rearguard and cause a traffic jam of players in a packed goalmouth at Ibrox

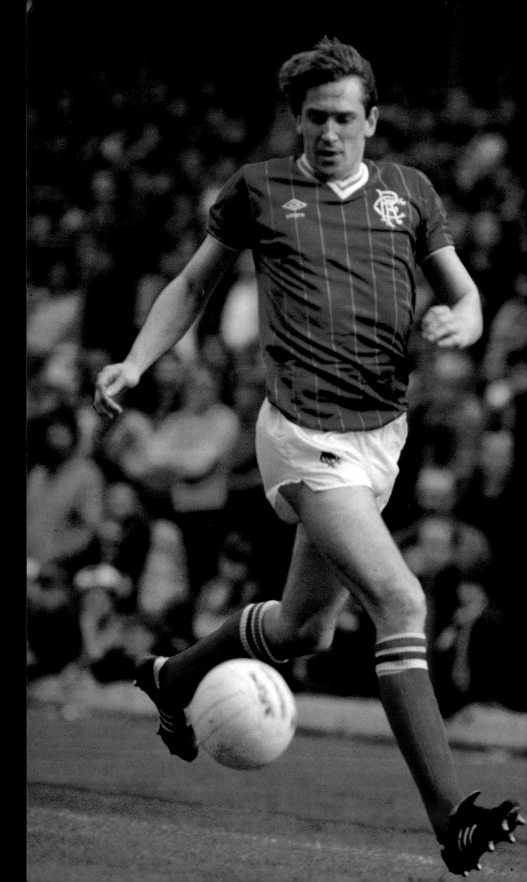

soon as you have brought it under control. Maybe even before you have had time to do that!

They harry you immediately, trying to force you into mistakes. It makes life hard for a defender and, while I was slightly apprehensive about the European games, I found them easier than I had expected. It had been a step into the unknown for me – but the unknown eventually didn't hold too many terrors.

Apart from the injury I suppose the two Cup final defeats hurt me a lot last season. Again, I felt for the supporters, especially in the Scottish Cup Final against Aberdeen at Hampden. They were tremendous that day. OK, I know that there are times when the Ibrox fans can be very critical of the team. That's their right. But that day I think they knew that we had done everything to give them the result they wanted.

I mean, we had been written off and yet, in the end, might have won the game. You know, despite all Aberdeen's success in Europe, I didn't feel afraid of them. I always thought that if Jim Bett and Robert Russell played as well as they could we would be in with a tremendous chance. They did and we were until the last minutes of extra time.

Apart from the result, I enjoyed the Cup final. I think that it should be the kind of gala day that everyone enjoys, players and fans alike. I had thought I would be nervous. But while I felt it a little bit at Ibrox where we all met before going to the game that had gone by the time I reached Hampden. Then all I could think about was the game and the telephone message I had from my old Hibs team-mate, goalkeeper Jim McArthur who said simply: 'Just go there and enjoy it because it's one of the big occasions in football.'

It's the way it turned out and these supporters helped make it for me. They were as disappointed as we were but they stayed there on the Hampden terracings cheering us even though we had lost the game. And lost the Cup, the one trophy we could still have won last season.

We will make it up to them. The players are all determined to land a major honour this season. Basically the side is still young, remember, and there is a lot of pressure attached to playing for Rangers. I feel it quite a bit on occasions, but it sharpens my appetite for the game. When you are ambitious and want to win and you go into a game knowing that people

*Opposite*: Skipper John McClelland, the man who follows in the footsteps of some of the greatest names in Scottish football, the players who have had the proud honour to captain Glasgow Rangers

are expecting you to take two points, you are keyed up. It's a pressure which some players will never experience.

Players from lesser clubs can go through their whole careers and all that people want are a few good results scattered through the season; enough to help them remain in the Top Ten, maybe enough to give them a run in the League Cup and the Scottish Cup. Maybe, if they are starting to get ambitious in a limited way, a chance to get into one of the European tournaments. But for most of them that is a dream – for Rangers it is something that they expect season after season. It's almost unthinkable for the team not to be in Europe and you soon learn to adapt to the pressure which is placed on you.

Certainly there is no way that you can simply shrug off a bad result or a string of bad results. The criticism can be wild if that happens. We had to face up to it last season when our mid-season form flopped and our League challenge dropped away. We want to avoid that this season. It was a three-horse race last year – well we want to be in on it this time. We want to be there at the last gasp of the season along with Dundee United, Celtic and Aberdeen. We don't want a gap widening between ourselves and the leaders the way it did last year.

Billy Stark, sold by St Mirren to Aberdeen in the close season, is foiled here by the long legs of Craig Paterson who moves in swiftly to clear in a Love Street meeting between the two teams

It won't be easy because the standards in the League are high. Personally I rate Aberdeen as the toughest opponents of all. And last year we broke even with them in the League matches. They beat us twice and we beat them twice. Their Cup final win edged them ahead. . . .

But they are a very strong all-round side and Mark McGhee is one of those centre forwards who try to drag you about, pull you out of position. The kind I don't relish playing against. McGhee and Frank McGarvey of Celtic are a bit the same in that respect. They don't play up against you all the time, they move around, darting here and there but still posing a threat all the time. They take you into areas where you don't want to go. I always prefer playing against a straightforward type of striker. Someone like Doug Somner, for example, who battles away with the centre half. But I suppose you can't win them all.

Swedish star Robert Prytz demonstrates the urgency Rangers showed in Paterson's European debut against the West German cracks Borussia Dortmund. Here Prytz leaves defender Lothe Huber trailing as he bursts clear

A portrait of £200,000 buy Craig Paterson who joined Rangers from Hibs

What I do want to win, though, is an honour with the club. If I'd stayed with Hibs being in two finals in the one season plus playing in Europe, would have been enough for me. Not any more. I want medals. I want to win. And I want to get myself back on the international scene. Last season the Scotland boss Jock Stein named me as an over-age player in the Under-21 side. I had to call off because of that injury. I'd like to think that he will give me my chance again this season. The international scene is important and the Under-21s have had a tremendous run over the past few seasons. It would be nice to get the chance to help them march into the later stages of the European Championships for the third time in succession.

But, having said all that, Rangers come first. I owe them a lot. They have given me my chance. It's up to me to repay them and that can only be done with regular success, for the club and for the supporters.

52

# THOSE FINAL DEFEATS

The season which ended for Rangers last summer with that extra time goal from Aberdeen striker Eric Black in the Scottish Cup Final, was one of misery.

For that defeat from the team which had conquered the best in Europe in the Cup Winners' Cup competition was the second time in the season that they had lost a final, and their league form had stuttered and stammered after a fine beginning.

Looking back it was difficult to believe that the team which had kicked off the year with a run of more than twenty games without defeat should end up empty-handed. Yet that is what happened.

Elsewhere in this book manager John Greig and others explain about the shattering blow to morale which came when the team went out of the UEFA Cup to Cologne in West Germany. That is a point of view with which I can sympathize. Until then Rangers had played with flair and imagination. Their new look team had been praised universally for their adventurous and yet organized approach.

Then with the defeat in Germany and the injury to Craig Paterson their dreams died.

One man certainly does not make a team. But in the case of Paterson there had been a new solidity about the back four since he arrived. Few goals had been lost as the former Hibs player lined up alongside Irishman John McClelland at the heart of the Ibrox defence. They stood there together blocking the way for even the best of the Scottish strikers.

When they travelled to Pittodrie and beat Aberdeen it was as if they had won the League already. The fans celebrated wildly as their team laid the jinx which had haunted them for eight miserable years.

Not since December 1974 had Rangers won a League game at Pittodrie. Striker Derek Johnstone was the sole survivor from the team which had won before. He scored then, along with Tommy McLean, now the Ibrox assistant manager, and he scored this time around too. The other Rangers goal came from

Striker Sandy Clark, whose goal put Rangers into the final, wins this aerial battle with Motherwell defender Johannes Edvaldsson

Robert Prytz, while Aberdeen had to settle for a penalty from Gordon Strachan as consolation.

Afterwards as the Rangers supporters stayed on the terracing to salute the victory, Johnstone told me: 'Now people will be able to stop talking about a jinx up here. It was great to end that run . . . because it gets to players when there is always talk of having a bogey ground.

'It doesn't matter how hard you try to put it out of your mind, it sticks there and it affects you. I mean this no-win sequence at Pittodrie went back before the Premier League had even started!

'I think this will show people that we are on the right lines now, that we are poised to do well in the League championship race.'

That was the way it looked that day at the end of September. But by the turn of the year the Rangers challenge had faded away once more. Ravaged by injuries, bruised by the beating in Cologne the team never did recover the fluency they had shown in those early heady months.

Sure, towards the end of the season they proved themselves difficult to beat. Only Dundee United and Celtic beat them in the run in to the season's end. But, by then, the team had ceased to score goals. Sandy Clark was bought from West Ham and added some power up front but he suffered from a nagging groin strain and the best is yet to come from the former Airdrie striker.

As John Greig pointed out: 'We missed a bundle of chances in the second half of the season. Some of them were unbelievable. If we had taken half a dozen of the easier ones then it could have made a difference of possibly ten points to our league total. Check that out and you'll find I'm right. We have to take more of the chances we make and having Sandy Clark up there is going to give us added finishing strength next season.'

The League soon become a memory and even when Celtic faced Rangers in the League Cup final in December the chances of the Ibrox men becoming champions were almost nil. But that Hampden game might have given them their first trophy of the season. . . .

They had shown good form in the League Cup and in two epic semi-final clashes with Hearts they had come out as four to one winners. It was a result which pleased the fans over the two games. It was too easy to describe Hearts as only a First Division team. They had experienced players blended with several outstanding youngsters. And they had a support which was better than almost any team in Scotland outside the Old Firm and, perhaps, Aberdeen. As Greig pointed out: 'As far as I'm concerned I'm playing against a Premier League outfit. They have that kind of professionalism and ambition about them and we won't take them lightly.'

He was right to say that. Hearts were bolstered by a management team of Alex MacDonald and Sandy Jardine – both still playing, and both well aware of the strengths and weaknesses of their former Ibrox team-mates. They had veteran winger Willie Johnston playing too to give their side an Ibrox flavour which spelled danger to Greig's men.

Not only that, they also brought a huge support to Ibrox for the first leg of the semi-final. As Rangers pointed out later it was the biggest travelling support outside of Celtic to visit the new-look stadium. Seven thousand fans came from Edinburgh and twenty-two and a half thousand watched the match which Rangers won 2-0. They scored first with a Davie Cooper goal and then late in the game Jim Bett gave them a vital second to put them in command for the second leg. But Hearts had stretched their Premier League opponents. They had done enough to show that Greig's pre-match assessment of their ability was correct and with MacDonald and Jardine planning for the return it was not going to be an easy passage to Hampden for the Ibrox men.

Davie Cooper runs into trouble against a couple of old team-mates. In the League Cup semi-final ex-Ibrox pair Alex MacDonald and Sandy Jardine join forces to stop the Rangers winger

Just under nineteen-thousand fans packed Tynecastle for the return and here Rangers showed their Cup fighting qualities. A penalty goal from Jim Bett pushed the tie beyond Hearts' reach and while Derek O'Connor did score for the Edinburgh men there was never any way that the tie was going to go their way. Instead eight minutes from the end Derek Johnstone added another to give Rangers a double victory.

It had been a hard semi-final and it had proved that Hearts would be worthy members of the Premier League the following season. It had also given Rangers the chance to win a trophy – the one they held from the previous season – and qualify for Europe early.

It didn't work out that way. In a Hampden Park where the crowd had been cut to fifty-five thousand because of reconstruction work, the form Rangers tried to recapture eluded them. Craig Paterson played but was not 100 per cent fit. The gamble taken by John Greig and the player failed. Charlie Nicholas and Murdo MacLeod scored before half time as Rangers trailed unconvincingly.

A glorious free kick goal from Jim Bett beat Pat Bonner early in the second half, but that was all Rangers could muster. Celtic had taken the first major honour of the season and Rangers,

It used to be an Old Firm confrontation – but here Rangers striker Colin McAdam is up against Hearts and one time Celtic centre half Roddy McDonald

even this early, were left thinking about Scottish Cup glory because the League had moved away from them.

Over the years the Scottish Cup has been good to Rangers. They had been in the final seven times in succession and as they marched through the early rounds, against lesser opposition, it looked as if they might still salvage something from a season of disappointment.

It took them two games to dispose of St Mirren in the semi-final. In the first at Celtic Park they should have won easily. In spite of Saints' protestations beforehand that they were going to escape the tag of 'the nearly men' of Scottish soccer, there was little challenge from them. Manager Ricky McFarlane admitted ruefully: 'We froze again. I didn't think that we would do that after being in the semi-finals last year and taking Aberdeen to a replay. But we did.'

They survived because of missed chances by Rangers but in the replay Sandy Clark struck and Rangers were through to meet the Aberdeen side which had swept victoriously through Europe. By then the scalp of Bayern Munich was hanging at Pittodrie after an epic European victory over the West German aces. Before the final itself, Real Madrid also became victims of Alex Ferguson's Aberdeen side and they came to Hampden as clear favourites.

But Rangers had beaten them at Ibrox in a Premier League game a few weeks earlier. That was a result which would cost Aberdeen their chance of the title and it gave confidence to Rangers as they approached the final.

No one gave them much hope against a team which had been described as a 'new force in Europe' after that Gothenburg final. Rangers seemed to be going along simply as victims.

But Grieg snarled beforehand: 'There is no way that Rangers go into finals simply to make up the numbers. We go into them looking for victories. We are not concerned about what Aberdeen have done in Europe. Like everyone else in Scotland we were delighted that they won the trophy – but now we want to stop them. And we can!'

Ferguson meanwhile worried whether there would be any reaction from the win in Sweden. But a stunning win over Hibs in their last League game proved that there wasn't and he came to Glasgow promising his fans that this Cup was just as important as the European Cup Winners' trophy.

Most of the work had ended at Hampden, the capacity had been increased and in spite of the lure of live television, sixty-three thousand people were in the great Glasgow ground for the final.

This is the sight Rangers fans would have liked to see at Hampden in the League Cup final against Celtic – here young Kenny Black is embraced by teenager Andy Kennedy after scoring in the League match at Ibrox. Rangers, though, eventually lost this match 2–1

Gordon Smith made history as the man who played in two finals in two different countries in the same season. Brought back on loan from Brighton he played for Rangers against Celtic in the League Cup final and then went on to Wembley with Brighton. Here he is in action against St Mirren

Burly striker Derek Johnstone scored against Hearts in the League Cup semi-final. Here he is out of luck as Celtic keeper Pat Bonner foils him in Celtic's 3–2 win at Parkhead

Veteran Peter McCloy who looked so good in the Cup final makes an instinctive edge of the box save against League champions Dundee United at Tannadice

It began as everyone had forecast with Aberdeen powering into attacks which constantly worried Rangers. It was in that period that Peter McCloy, the veteran recalled to action earlier in the year, came to Rangers' rescue with some splendid saves.

Then gradually the game turned. Rangers started to win the battle of the midfield. Robert Russell outplayed little Gordon Strachan, Jim Bett controlled his area and the tide turned. Before the end it was Rangers who almost snatched the trophy with a thundering shot from Bett which somehow Scotland keeper Jim Leighton reached and turned over the bar. What celebrations that would have brought!

Then in extra time little Billy Davies did have the ball in the net but a foul was given against him. And so Eric Black broke the deadlock with only minutes remaining and the Cup was taken back to Aberdeen.

But the memory which remained with the Rangers players was of their support staying to cheer them as they collected their runners-up medals. Normally Greig refuses to allow them to take a lap of honour after defeat. This time he broke his own rule and the players went over to salute the thousands who saluted them. It was an emotional moment at the end of a season of sadness.

# MY YEAR OF AGONY
# by John Greig

It was a hard year for John Greig. A year when he had to survive the kind of criticism which would have broken lesser men. A year when he saw his team reach two major domestic finals and yet know within himself that they had failed because winning is the one thing which matters to Rangers. For other teams it is an achievement to reach one final. To Rangers it means nothing unless there is victory at the end of it all.

No one has to tell Greig that. He learned it as a player, learned it from the first days he stepped into Ibrox as a teenager more than twenty years ago. Now in the manager's chair he remembers the lesson.

That big, impressive desk where Bill Struth once sat is the point where the buck stops and Greig accepts that. But he is always a man to face up to his critics, whether they attack him from the front or whether they snipe from the sidelines. When you talk to him you soon realize that what sustains him most in times of trouble is the deep respect he has for the Rangers Football Club – for its traditions, for its past and for its future, for its players and for its supporters.

Most of the time last season he suffered in silence. His thoughts remained private as the team staggered through a loss of form which no one could have predicted. But now in this face to face interview Greig talks of the problems he has had as a manager, and makes it plain that he will never run away from those problems. . . .

GALLACHER – By most club's standards the past season would have been a success. You reached the final of the League Cup where you lost by an odd goal. You reached the final of the Scottish Cup and again lost by an odd goal, this one coming in extra time. You also qualified for Europe by being fourth in the League. Yet for Rangers it was a black season, a troubled one. How do you explain this?

GREIG – It's simple enough to explain why these achievements aren't enough. Rangers fans expect success. They want to see the team winning trophies. It's a tremendous record having

62

Dave McKinnon, one of the new signings who settled in quickly to become a fans favourite

Robert Russell, the best play-maker in Scottish football, according to Ibrox boss John Greig

63

Rangers manager John Greig – he spent many
lonely nights last season as his team's
challenge crumbled in the major competitions

been in eight successive Scottish Cup Finals. But they wanted
us to win them all.

I don't blame them for that. That's the way this club is and
it would be a lesser club if it allowed that kind of attitude to
wither away. But it's nothing new to me. I've played here in
teams which won 'trebles', the team which won the European
Cup Winners' Cup, too. But never at any time were we allowed
to sit back and be content with what we had already done. No.
Whenever the trophies had been won we knew that the next
competition we played in had to be won as well.

It's the way it has always been and even though it is more
difficult now to win year after year it's still the way the supporters think and I'm not going to disagree with them. It's the
way Rangers players should think too.

GALLACHER – You say it's more difficult now. Is that because
of the higher standards of play in the Premier League. There is
no doubt that there have been vast improvements in tactics and
technique over the past six or seven years.

One of the teenage discoveries of last season, lanky striker Andy
Kennedy who played for the Scotland Under-18 team

GREIG – Well, that is the reason. Other teams have come
through and made their bids for power. It used to be between
ourselves and Celtic. For nine long years we had to play on
while Celtic were taking the title time after time. No one else
really butted in to take up the challenge for us. Briefly a team
would appear and then they would just drop out again. We had
to fight that battle ourselves.

And when we achieved some success Celtic were fighting it
out with us for most of the time. Now you have two fresh
contenders for the honours – Dundee United as champions and
Aberdeen as Cup holders and European Cup Winners' Cup
holders. When would you have thought that possible? Neither
ourselves nor Celtic were able to lift either of the major trophies.
Celtic got the League Cup and were runners-up in the League.
But the point I am making is this: there is a whole new ball
game on out there in the Premier League.

Dundee United and Aberdeen have been picking up honours
over the past few years and they will want to continue to do

that. The days of a two-club domination of the Scottish scene have gone for the moment. What we have to do is break up the challenge from the northeast clubs and fight it out with Celtic at the same time.

GALLACHER – The two clubs you mention, Dundee United and Aberdeen, have gained their success mainly with home-grown talent. I know that you are trying to do the same. How close are you?

GREIG – I'm getting there. You are now seeing the fruits of the youth policy I started. It takes time to bring young players on but Dave McPherson came through magnificently last season. Billy Davies was good enough to come on as a sub in the Cup final.

We also had Andy Kennedy playing for a spell in the first team and there were times when we had half a dozen teenagers in the side at the one time.

GALLACHER – You say it takes time and Jim McLean of Dundee United has always maintained that it has taken him ten years to build his side. Alex Ferguson says it takes six or seven years to get players through the system. Is your problem that you don't have time on your side?

GREIG – I suppose that is one problem. Both Aberdeen and Dundee United could afford to have bad spells, seasons without winning a major honour and no one would think any the less of them. But, as I've already stressed, Rangers have to keep on winning. Celtic, to be fair, have the same kind of situation to contend with.

It doesn't make it easy at all. You can't rush young players in any case. Take Andy Kennedy last season. He did marvellously well for us in a period when we had been hit by injuries. He had to play on and on. Even when I knew that it was time to spell him, to give him a break, I had to persist. At the end of the season the laddie was drained. That's the kind of risk you don't want to take with them even though sometimes you have to.

This season Andy will be back in the first team every now and again. He will be given the chance to develop in the reserves. That's where he can learn his trade best. But he has enough talent and pace to get into the first team. We will use him in certain games but we don't want to overplay him. He has to take a rest every now and again. It's the only thing to do.

With some of the others it will be different. The players who have been in the reserves for a few seasons now will have to start to show us that they are ready for the first team. They can't stay on in the second team and block the progress of other youngsters. They have to give notice to us that they are knocking at the door. Some of them will be doing that. The goalkeeper Andy Bruce, for instance, has been outstanding in the reserves and in the Scotland youth team. And Kenny Lyall, Kenny Black and little Billy Davies will have to get themselves into the reckoning this year.

GALLACHER – The conveyor belt of talent appears to be working OK now. Did these lads bring you success last season in the second team?

GREIG – Yes, it was these boys who won the Premier League reserve title. I didn't use too many of the experienced men at all. I relied on the youngsters and they won it. That says something for them – but they have to take the step up now. They have to look at big Davie McPherson and say to themselves, 'If he can do it then we can do it too.'

Too many times in the past at Ibrox I've felt that young players came along and then weren't given enough chances. They didn't get into the first team and they found it hard to get into the reserves because first team pool men dominated there. I have vowed that won't happen with me. Any laddie will get the opportunity here to make the grade.

This time Jim Bett, one of the best players Greig has seen at Ibrox, loses out to a challenge from Hearts' young midfield star Dave Bowman

Perhaps it was this kind of Premier League tackling which made Swedish star Robert Prytz want to return to the Continent. He is felled here by Motherwell's Stuart Rafferty

GALLACHER – How young do you go after these players nowadays? It used to be around sixteen or seventeen and then it dropped lower. Where is it now?

GREIG – Would you believe that we have boys coming in here at twelve and thirteen years old. I have just started off a team of Under-15 players who will play at Benburb Juniors' ground in one of the Glasgow leagues. A man called Bobby Dinnie will be running the side and already he has some great players coming through for us. He is one of the best signings I've made. I don't think he needs any more recommendation than to say he helped discover and groom Kenny Dalglish as a youngster.

Bobby has tremendous contacts and he will have this side as a nursery for us. Other laddies that little bit older will be going out to other juvenile clubs we use to bring boys on until they can join the ground staff. But I'm excited about this new outfit. It's something that I have been wanting to do since I took over as manager but there were a whole host of other things to attend to and I also wanted the set up to be right. I think that this *is* right. I'm sure it is, in fact. The future is going to be safe.

GALLACHER – How badly did you take the criticism which was levelled at you last season?

GREIG – No one likes to be criticized. Let me say that straight-away. I don't believe there is a single person on this earth who likes the kind of criticism which I had to suffer. Some of it may have been justified. I suppose I have to accept that if I didn't win these supporters a major trophy then I do deserve to be criticized. But others weren't as fair and there were times when I might have answered them. But I didn't because that is not the way a manager of Rangers should conduct himself.

I've been with this club a long time. It's been my life and I've watched and I've listened and I've learned. There is a code of conduct here especially where the manager is concerned. He is expected to behave with a certain dignity and I have tried to follow that role. Certainly it's been hard to stay quiet when, at times, I've known that the criticism has been unfair. Or that something being mentioned as fact is not true. But it just isn't the Rangers way to get involved in slanging matches and that's the way I've played it.

It has hurt all right. The results sometimes hurt too. I know how the fans feel. I have felt the same way myself. There were Saturday nights last season when I went straight home from a game, got into my track suit and just sat in the house watching the telly. I couldn't face going out because the disappointment was so intense.

The fans are the same, I'm sure. They like to get out on a Saturday if the team has won, get down to the pub, have a few drinks, a wee bit of a celebration, a talk about the game. When they lose it's a night ruined. There were a few of my nights ruined too, believe me.

GALLACHER – Obviously you feel deeply about the fans and about not giving them the success they demand. You don't criticize them too much for maybe jeering you or hammering you. Why is that?

GREIG – Look, it's their right to have their say because Rangers is their team. I can't promise to pick the team they want every week. I can't promise to please them all the time. That's impossible so I know that I'll be moaned about because this player or that player is left out. You have to accept that.

Similarly, you have to accept that if a mistake is made in a team selection or in tactics then you have to carry the can for that too. That is a part of the job.

But what I always remember is that sixty-five thousand of these supporters turned out to honour me in my testimonial game when I ended my playing career. They did that I suppose because they knew that as a player I would give everything I had for the club. I'm still the same way. I'm still the same man. I still give everything for the club. That will never change.

Maybe I've made mistakes – which manager hasn't? But no one will ever be able to accuse me of running away from this job. I'm no quitter. I never jibbed when things were hard as a player and I'm not going to jib now. I don't think the supporters would expect me to do that.

I know what I want to achieve here and I know that the foundations are being laid to bring this club back to the top. The sooner that happens the better.

GALLACHER – You had to make a lot of changes last season, a lot of new faces were in and a lot of old faces went out. Did this harm the team?

GREIG – I did think that there would be some harm done. The team had been together a long time and suddenly it had to go. I couldn't keep the Old Guard forever. That wasn't right and I had been criticized for it.

I had to change things and I did so. Any other team would have been given a longer transitional period than us. But I've already explained that side of it. We were also asked to achieve a whole lot of things when injuries caused us to suffer badly. There were times when the treatment room looked more like a clearing station for a battlefield than part of a football club.

The serious injuries we had included Craig Paterson who seemed jinxed after joining us, Ally Dawson who eventually came back to international form, and Robert Russell who, for me, is the finest play-maker in the country. In fact, I'd just ask people to remember his Cup final appearance against Aberdeen. He was the best man on the park.

Anyhow, we also had injuries to Derek Johnstone, Colin McAdam, Gordon Dalziel and Robert Prytz.

Time after time we had to re-cast the team and the understanding we had built up in the early part of the season went

70

The kind of bad luck in front of goal which dogged Rangers through the season as John MacDonald beats Pat Bonner only for the ball to hit the post in the 0–0 draw at Celtic Park

for a burton. I'm not making excuses here. I'm simply pointing out what happened.

GALLACHER – If it's any consolation to you, Jim McLean told me that if his team had suffered the same string of injuries which plagued you then they wouldn't have taken the title.

GREIG – It's good of Jim to say that. We were badly hit and there was nothing we could do because several of the injuries were really serious. It wasn't a case of missing a player for a week or two. One Saturday I only had nineteen fit players and two games to play. Six youngsters had to be drafted into the reserves that weekend.

GALLACHER – I suppose that is part of the explanation for your inconsistency?

GREIG – Yes, but only a part of it. We have shown too much inconsistency over the past few seasons. We have proved in Cup competitions, in one-off games that we can match the best in the country. Then we slip in the League. That has been our downfall – and it's not good enough.

We have to mount a real challenge in the Premier League this time around. That is the prize the fans want most and we can't afford the kind of slip-ups we have had in the past. Every team sags a little at one time or another. Celtic have done it . . .

Dundee United and Aberdeen have done it . . . but our trouble has been that the bad spells have gone on too long. That cannot continue to happen.

GALLACHER – You are losing Jim Bett for next season and perhaps Robert Prytz. Is this a blow to you?

GREIG – Losing Jim Bett is a terrible blow. As far as I'm concerned he is one of the best players who has been at Ibrox in the twenty odd years that I've been here. The trouble was that Jim, although he was a Rangers supporter, could not settle back in Glasgow. Or, at least, his wife who is from Iceland couldn't settle. It made him unhappy and so he had to go back to Belgium.

There was nothing we could do about it. Last season we saw Jim at his best in only about half the games we played because his domestic worries were getting to him. We couldn't go on that way. For me it's a tragedy that we have lost him. Robert Prytz didn't seem to settle too well either and when he came back after playing for Sweden he told me that he wanted to go back to the Continent. That was that.

Anyhow, what I want here are players who know what this club is about. I want players who know what it means to come into that entrance hall, who feel something for the tradition of the club, who respect the blue jersey they are asked to wear. I know that might sound corny to some people – but it doesn't sound corny to me even after all the years I've been in the game. It's important to me and I want it all to be important to the players. I want them to climb onto the team bus and sing all the club songs just as we used to do when I was a player. I want them to be aware of the tradition that they are a part of. Bringing up your own players helps with that.

GALLACHER – Does that mean you have stopped buying players?

GREIG – No, You don't shut a door completely. There are times, as I said earlier, when you have to buy players to augment a squad. All the other top teams in the country have done it after all.

I'm looking to strengthen the squad now. I'm always looking to strengthen the squad. There has been a lot of money spent but there has also been a lot of money taken in. We have sold well too. The books have been, to a great extent, balanced.

I'll tell you one thing I've learned as a manager. If I make a mistake in buying a player then I'll let that player move on. I'll just sell him to another club. That's the way the game is. There is no use dwelling on mistakes and hoping that they will come right. I won't be afraid to do that now or in the future.

72

Full back Ally Dawson was an injury victim early in the year, but a return to form was followed by a recall to the international team for the Paisley-born player

But what I want to do is buy players who want to play for this club. I think my two buys last season proved that they wanted to . . . could you doubt Dave McKinnon or Craig Paterson? They'd die for this club. . . .

That's what we need. We have to get that attitude in the whole side so that any inconsistency can be beaten. We have to be able to shrug off a defeat and come back after it and win a victory. There is no use lying down in defeat . . . we did that to a certain extent last season.

GALLACHER – Are you talking about the Cologne game?

GREIG – That and the Old Firm game which was directly before it. We were leading in that game until very late in the match. We were drawing 2-2 with ninety seconds to go and we lost it. Then we were hit by that hammering in West Germany. That scarred the team. The psychological battering from those two matches plus the injuries we had picked up demoralized the players. But we can't afford to have that happen again. We have to pick ourselves up from defeats and get on with things.

That is the kind of Rangers team I want. And I want to see it this season!

These fans who supported us at Hampden in the final against Aberdeen deserve that. I gave everything as a player and I'm giving the same as a manager. The fans are the last people in this world that I want to let down.

It's a shot for goal from Robert Russell as he sends the ball flying for the target despite a late intervention from Celtic full back Mark Reid

# BREAKTHROUGH TO THE FIRST TEAM
## by Dave McPherson

It seems to happen a lot these days. Young players are tempted to go down south and join one of the top English outfits.

I suppose it has always been that way to some extent but with English football being shown so much on telly in Scotland the attraction is now probably greater. But it didn't affect me one bit – at least, not after I was told that Rangers wanted to sign me.

A portrait of teenager Dave McPherson who made his first-team breakthrough at Ibrox last season

Young Dave McPherson says he wants to improve on his heading. He seems to be doing all right here as he clears from Motherwell striker Andy Harrow

Once I had heard that, no other club could possibly interest me. I wouldn't have cared if it had been Liverpool or Manchester United or anyone else. The one place I wanted to play was Ibrox. I did have offers from clubs in the south. They wanted me to go down to train and then to sign for them. Some were tempting, or might have been in different circumstances.

But the simple fact is that I'd always been a Rangers supporter. They were the team I followed when I was at school in Glasgow and it had always been my ambition to play for them.

I was playing for my school team, Crookston Castle, in the mornings and for Pollok United in the afternoons when Rangers first saw me. They must have watched me fairly regularly and then the manager Mr Greig came to see me and asked me to join the ground staff. I jumped at the chance and immediately I joined up at Ibrox I was promoted to playing for the Pollok Under-18 team.

I stayed there with them until Rangers asked me to go full time after I had been given some more experience with Gartcosh United. That was two years ago – it seems like yesterday. Yet, in that time I have managed to make the breakthrough that I dreamed about when I was still a kid at Crookston Castle – the breakthrough to the Ibrox first team.

It was a dream back then. It was a dream when I went onto the ground staff. But even at the beginning of last season the dream still seemed very far off as far as I was concerned.

Sure, I'd been able to make the Scotland youth team squad and I'd been playing regularly in the reserves. I'd even made the squad which travelled to France for the pre-season tournament at Lille.

The progress I had made was steady without being spectacular and the problem which now reared up in front of me was obvious. Just before the trip to France the club had gone into the transfer market and signed Craig Paterson from Hibs. As well as that, John McClelland had slotted into a central defensive role the year before and had built a tremendous reputation with his performances for Northern Ireland in the World Cup. Big John had been one of the outstanding Irish players in a run which took them into the second phase of the competition.

If that wasn't competition enough there were signs that Derek Johnstone and Colin McAdam, both of whom were able to play either centre forward or centre half, might opt for defensive roles.

That didn't make the future look quite so rosy for yours truly. The word from the Boss, however, and from all the others on the backroom staff, was encouraging. They thought that I was developing along the lines they wanted.

And the grounding you get at Ibrox doesn't allow you time to sit down and feel sorry for yourself. You are taught to face up to challenges, to be ready to fight for your place if things seem to be going against you, and never to let your head go down.

As far as I was concerned I still had time on my side. I hadn't expected to be in the first team squad quite so soon. As I said earlier, it seemed only yesterday that I was playing with Gartcosh and travelling with the Rangers youth teams to play in the Croix tournament.

That was one of the highlights of joining up at Ibrox. Every year the club sends off their younger players to take part in that competition. It's only in a small village not far from Lille where the first team played last summer. But because we have been going so regularly over the years it has become a home from home for so many of the players. The experience you get from playing there is fantastic. It's when you play against teams from South America, from Spain and Portugal and Italy and West Germany and France and also from Russia and other Iron Curtain countries that you realize just how much there is to learn about the game of football.

No matter how hard you try on your own, or just playing away matches in Scotland it's hard to grasp the differences in style.

It is only when you are there that you can learn. It's the most invaluable piece of training I had at Ibrox in my earlier days. You have to find out how to cope with these various styles. You learn when to tackle and when it is best to try to jockey an opponent. You see how they try to build up their attacks from the back – a lesson which was not lost on me.

Being a 'sweeper' myself I found that of particular interest and value. I think that the Continental teams do this more than we do in Britain. Down through the years there have been some marvellous foreign players who played as 'sweepers' with their club and at international level.

There are two favourites of mine – Rudi Krol who played with Ajax and Holland and Franz Beckenbauer who was with Bayern Munich and West Germany. They were the masters. Anyone who plays in the position that I do alongside the centre half must look at them and say, 'That is the highest standard you can get,' and then the problem is trying to emulate them. Both were tremendous passers of the ball. They could play it long and they could play it short and always they would play it with accuracy. Any chance I get of watching them on film I take because no one is better than they were.

Krol was still showing his skills last season when he played for Holland against Scotland at Hampden!

The Boss has likened me to Alan Hansen of Liverpool. He did that one day soon after I started my run in the first team. I had come through from defence, played a one-two with someone and then strode on to score against Dundee.

The lanky figure of Dave McPherson, wearing the number five jersey on the extreme right of the picture turns away from goal after scoring for Rangers for the first time. It was against Dundee and had manager John Greig comparing the youngster to Liverpool star Alan Hansen

Not quite so bright for young McPherson here as Davie Bell hits Dundee's equaliser and the Rangers defender is stranded

Another of the young players who go back to Ibrox in the afternoons, youth cap Andy Kennedy here in action against Celtic defender Graeme Sinclair

Well, it was nice of him to say so but I know that I still have a lot of work to do before I can be really satisfied with my game. In the sense that I like to get forward, like to be up there helping set up attacks then I'm like Hansen. But I still go back to Ibrox in the afternoons to work on the parts of my game which I feel need brushing up. I work hard at my passing because I want that to be better. There is a lot of work to be done on my left foot still. And I work hard on my heading because that has to be improved. I do a lot of these things at training in the morning, but almost every afternoon I go back to Ibrox and work on the particular things I feel I have to improve. I concentrate on them exclusively in these afternoon work outs and the great thing is that we are all enouraged to go back for that extra training. It has helped a lot of the lads at Ibrox. Most afternoons I'm there with the likes of Billy Davies, Kenny Black and Andy Kennedy and sometimes some of the others. If we're not working at the individual skills then we'll be playing a bit of head tennis on the court under the main stand. Then, when we really want to work we go across to the training ground at the Albion. That's where the important stuff is done. Passing with both feet, heading, close control, all the things that can make you a better player. For instance, as I said, my left foot needs more work. So does my heading. I have made some improvement there but I need to be more powerful when I'm challenging in the air so I work hard at that. There are times, too, when I lose concentration during a game and that has to be conquered.

Writing about it this way must make it seem a lot of hard work to people outside the game. In a way it is – but I enjoy every moment of it. That's why I'm there for the extra training because I genuinely enjoy myself. The main aim is to make yourself a better player, and that's what I want above all else.

The season just past turned out to be a brilliant one as far as I was concerned. Starting off with the trip to France, being on the substitutes' bench in Cologne and then coming into the first team. Unhappily for Craig Paterson I got that chance after he was injured. But even when he was fit the manager kept me in the team. He reshuffled the back four around a little bit and by the time the Scottish Cup Final came around I was still in with Craig beside me and the skipper John McClelland going to left back, another position he has played in for Northern Ireland.

So even though it was a disappointment to lose in the final at Hampden it was still one of the great occasions of my career.

And, it was not only the final which crowned my season – I was chosen to play for the Scotland youth team in the World Championships in Mexico. It was always in my mind that I might manage to get a place in the squad, but I had been forced to pull out of the team which won the European title in Finland the year before.

Now here was the same squad going to Mexico and I thought that I might be left behind. But because I had made it into the Ibrox first team I made it to Mexico as well.

The youth team coach Andy Roxburgh described me as the most improved young player in Scotland – quite a compliment when you consider the other players from the Premier League in the pool such as Celtic midfield man Paul McStay. And Eric Black and Neale Cooper from Aberdeen had been in the side which won the European Cup Winners' Cup against Real Madrid in Gothenburg.

Being a part of that trip was a bonus I had only dreamed of. But it was a season when at least some of my dreams came true.

All that was needed to complete things was success for the club. That, I'm sure will come.

Personally, though, it could scarcely have been better for me. Playing in the Premier League was a challenge in itself. It's a big step up from the reserves to the really fierce competition which exists in the Top Ten.

Then I was asked to play against the best players in the country . . . like Celtic striker Charlie Nicholas for one. By the end of the season everyone in Britain knew about Charlie because every top club wanted him.

I knew about him a little earlier than most and at closer quarters because I had to face him in my first Old Firm game. He is absolutely deadly in the box. Inside that eighteen-yard line I haven't seen a player who is more lethal than he is. You simply cannot relax when you are up against him. What is demanded from any defender is 100 per cent concentration through the entire ninety minutes. In fact, you probably need 110 per cent concentration if you are to stop him scoring.

He and the Aberdeen striker Mark McGhee were the most difficult opponents I had to face in the Premier League and for different reasons. Mark shields the ball magnificently and then lays it off so well. He is very strong and it is hard to get him off the ball. Mark is very good in that department of the game and his close control is tremendous. It's quite astonishing just how well he keeps the ball at his feet when you consider how powerful he is. Normally you expect that kind of dribbling from smaller players. But Mark has that knack along with the shielding ability that seems to be so important in the modern game. He was vitally important to Aberdeen last season and one very difficult opponent. I wasn't alone in thinking that. The Real Madrid sweeper Johnny Metgod must have felt the same way when he had to try to stop him in Gothenburg.

People always ask me what I would like most of all in my career. Well, I think I would like to be able to help Rangers win a major European trophy. We all took it badly last season when we went out of the UEFA Cup with that heavy defeat from Cologne. It didn't help that the West Germans had so many good players lined up against us. I think that Pierre Littbarski, Klaus Allofs and the young midfield man Stefan Engels were as good as any of the players I've seen in Europe. It simply hurt to go out when with some luck we could have been marching on alongside Dundee United, who reached the quarter-finals, and Aberdeen who won their competition.

Full back Kenny Black another of the Ibrox youngsters who team up
with Dave McPherson

Little midfielder Billy Davies, another Pollok United graduate, who joined up at Ibrox in the same season as McPherson. And he joined him on the field during the Scottish Cup Final, coming on as a substitute and having a goal disallowed!

I know what a boost it gave the game in Scotland when Aberdeen won in Gothenburg. And it would be tremendous if we could be the next team to pull it off. That's number one but I'd settle for any success for the club. Losing in two Cup finals at home last season was hard to take and by the odd goal in each one. That was the kind of season it was for us. We all want to do better and we all want to see the Cups sitting in the Trophy Room at Ibrox. On a personal level I'd like to stay in the first team, consolidate my position there, and then continue my progress with Scotland.

More and more you see players making the natural progression from the youth team, through to the Under-21 side and then on to the full international side. I'd like to follow that path some day myself.

Meantime I'll just keep working away on those extra afternoon sessions and hope that this season will be the lift off for some real success in my Ibrox career.

# HOW THE WORLD CUP CHANGED MY CAREER
## by John McClelland

I still find it hard to believe that I'm now captain of Glasgow Rangers, one of the great clubs of Europe. Not because I have any doubts about my ability to do the job they have asked me to do, but simply because a player who has knocked around the small club circuit rarely gets the chance to push himself into prominence with a big side. It is very easy to get lost in the lower leagues, easy to disappear, easy to become frustrated, disenchanted and then to drop your own standards and give up on any ambitions you might have had.

That could easily have happened to me. When I left Portadown as a youngster to join Cardiff City I felt that the world was opening up for me. Cardiff were in the Second Division then, they played in European football and they had several Welsh international players in their line up. Also instead of being a part-timer with Portadown here I was going into full-time football. It seemed the big break.

The money Cardiff paid wasn't big by British standards, but by Irish League standards it was fine. They gave Portadown £5000 in cash for my signature and then promised them another £5000 when I had played a certain number of first-team matches. The trouble was that Cardiff were relegated to the Third Division eighteen months after I joined them. If I played just a handful more games for them they had to fork out another £5000. Having just been relegated they had to cut their wage bill so several players were being handed free transfers. When they came to me they realized I was going to cost them five grand inside a few more games over and above any wages so I was axed too.

It seemed like the end of the world for me. I went back home to Ireland hoping that someone would come after me with a signing offer. All that happened was that a few clubs from the Republic of Ireland approached me and asked me to join them. But I thought that would be a step backwards in my career, going to a country which possibly had lower league standards than where I had started off in the Irish League with Portadown. It didn't sit right at all and so I continued to look around.

Basically I had tasted the kind of football I wanted to be involved in. OK, Cardiff wasn't any big deal, but other clubs were looking for players. I didn't want to disappear into a backwater – and that's what I felt I would be doing if I went back to an Irish club, no matter which side of the border it was on.

Yet even when I did sign for another club it was in a kind of backwater, but, in my eyes at least, it was closer to the mainstream of soccer. I returned to Wales to the non-league side Bangor City and back to part-time football. But somehow, even though I had to take a job as a hospital orderly, I felt that I had done the right thing.

I remember thinking to myself, 'At least I'm on the mainland and if people remember me from Cardiff they won't have to look too hard to find me again.'

Luckily that's the way it worked out. Bangor reached the final of the Welsh Cup which is a two-legged affair. We met Wrexham who had just been promoted and were getting a bit of publicity. Watching the games was Billy Bingham, now boss of Northern Ireland, but then the manager at Mansfield. I had been at Bangor three years when Billy saw me and bought me and that was the move which eventually became the springboard for the success I have managed to find so far.

You see, a year or so later, Billy Bingham fell out with the directors at Mansfield, left the job as team boss there and soon after was appointed manager of Northern Ireland. I'll always remain grateful to him for not forgetting me. He put me into the Irish pool and I've stayed there ever since.

And it was Billy who recommended me to the Rangers manager John Greig when he was looking for experienced defenders. At that time, in the summer of 1979, my contract with Mansfield was coming to an end and there was a lot of talk about various clubs coming in for me – clubs in England, I mean. It didn't cross my mind that I could finish up by playing in all four home countries at club level!

Spurs were mentioned, Stoke were linked with me as well, but when I came north with the Irish squad to play Scotland in a British International Championship game at Hampden, it was Rangers who stepped in to sign me. They agreed terms with Mansfield of around £90,000 and I was signed on the afternoon of the game against the Scots, just a few hours before the kick off.

Then after the match my Ibrox boss John Greig announced

Rangers skipper John McClelland shouts advice as he covers Dundee striker Eric Sinclair in this Premier League game

it to the press. I don't suppose too many of the Rangers fans had heard of me until then – and that was to cause me a lot of hurt before my first season with the club was over.

At the time, though, it didn't concern me. John Greig had watched me play, he had had others watch me and they were happy with what they had seen. That apart, I was holding down my place in the Northern Ireland team and playing in the World Cup qualifying ties. Maybe I was a relative unknown in Scotland but outside in the bigger world people knew who I was and knew that I was picking up 'caps' for my country.

Mind you, in another way I felt a bit strange about moving to Scotland because it had never entered my mind that a club from north of the border would come in for me. Of course, I knew about Rangers and about Celtic and all the great Scottish players but it had just not seemed likely that this was where I would continue my career. I had thought that I would stay in England, hopefully hoisting myself up a division or two in the process. But I'm glad that didn't happen because, in spite of the early troubles I had, I have enjoyed being with Rangers. And being made captain of the club last season was one of the biggest honours I could ever imagine.

But to get to these troubles. It seemed that I was jinxed in that first season. Off I went to Sweden to play in a few pre-season warm-up games which seemed the ideal way for me to settle in. Going over there, living with the rest of the lads and getting to know them, training and playing all the time was a good opportunity to develop an understanding with the other players. In theory it was the perfect opener for me. In practice it turned into a nightmare. In the second game of the tour I damaged my ankle ligaments so badly that I was out of action for almost two months. So the start of the season was wiped out. There was no way I could play and then, when I did get into the team, it was in time to be part of a European disaster!

Because of injuries to other players the Boss put me into the team at full back. Now I've played there before and I've played there since. But, remember this, the getting-to-know-you routine I had hoped to develop with the other players in Sweden hadn't taken place. This was us getting to know each other – on the field. In a European game.

Sorry, missed this time, John! The ball goes through to Scotland international keeper Billy Thomson as John McClelland, upfield helping his attack against St Mirren, fails to connect

The man who found that a World Cup made him an
Ibrox hero – John McClelland who was made
Rangers' captain last season

If I had been playing centre half, which is my favourite
position, then I might have cracked it. Instead, as I said, I was
at full back and I still hadn't got used to the defensive pattern
that the Rangers side used. I had a nightmare time and was
taken off. At the time John Greig thought that I had frozen a
little bit, playing in front of a big crowd in an important European game. It wasn't that – I'm not the type to freeze – it was
just that I had a really bad game. I knew it myself and there
was no way that I blamed the manager for hauling me off. It
was just the second in a series of bad luck stories which struck
me that first year.

Not too long after that I was injured again. Another nasty
one, done at training on a Friday morning and I was out for
months again. I needed an operation for that one and I couldn't
train at all. It took me a long time to get over it and for a spell
I thought that I was going to miss the World Cup trip with
Northern Ireland. I'd played in most of the qualifying games

and I was desperate to make the squad which was to be named in the spring.

Eventually, when the injury did clear, John Greig pushed me back into the first team, at centre half this time, and I stayed there and played until the Scottish Cup Final against Aberdeen. That spell was enough to convince Billy Bingham that I was ready for Spain too. Beforehand it had looked as if the injuries would mean me staying at home. Again, I would have understood the manager's position. He couldn't run the risk of going to Spain with one of his pool players unfit. After all, the Northern Ireland pool was pretty thin on the ground in any case.

Still it worked out and gave me the chance to answer the critics I had had to put up with since joining Rangers. I still don't know why it was but I became one of the butts on the local Radio Clyde phone-in on a Saturday after the games. People kept calling up and saying that John Greig should not have bought a player from the English Fourth Division. They kept saying that Rangers should be setting their sights higher. And one man who went on after an Old Firm game made it plain that he felt I simply wasn't good enough to play for Rangers.

As far as I could make out he was ready to hand out that abuse because I had missed a scoring chance in the game at Parkhead. He didn't criticize my defensive qualities in the game – and I felt it was one of my better games in that season.

That didn't seem to make any difference to the critics. They carped because they thought that Rangers should have been buying big name players and they didn't put me in that category. Also with my missing so many games through injury during the season I hadn't had the greatest of chances to convince anyone that I would fit into the Rangers set-up.

But the World Cup was to change all that. And I must admit I had a little bit of a go at some of these phone-in people when a few of the Scottish journalists visited me at the Irish hotel in Madrid. There we were, after all, in the second phase of the greatest competition in the world while the Scots were back home. And I had played in all three games, including the one in Valencia when we defeated Spain, the host nation, by one goal to nothing.

Eventually I played in all five Ireland games, two of them in Zaragoza, one in Valencia and then the last two in Madrid. It was a great experience for all of us. I don't think any of us thought that we would do so well. It isn't often that we Irish get to the finals, remember. I know that Scotland has had a lot

On guard! Skipper John McClelland and Ally Dawson stave off the
challenge from Celtic's Charlie Nicholas as Peter McCloy gathers this
ball in one of last season's Old Firm clashes. This one ended in a
goalless draw

of success in qualifying in recent times. You haven't failed since
1974 but we haven't had anything like that record so it was
important to us.

We drew with Yugoslavia, beat little Honduras by a single
goal and then beat Spain by the same margin. Each time Gerry
Armstrong scored. Then it was up to Madrid. We drew with
the Austrians but lost out in the end to the French who beat us
4-1 on a day when the temperature soared well over a hundred

Skipper John McClelland turns away, arm raised as he celebrates scoring against Motherwell. Striker Sandy Clark rushes in from the right of the picture to congratulate him

degrees. It was like playing in an oven . . . but I'm not making excuses. The French were a good team. It was a sad end, but none of us had expected to get that far so we had some consolation.

I had a personal consolation, too – the support I had from some of the fans who were there backing Northern Ireland but wearing their Rangers scarves. It was almost like having a personal little fan club following you and after the season I had gone through it was a big, big boost to me. It helped to give me the confidence to come back and really assert myself in the side. I felt that acceptance was on the way.

What I couldn't realize then was how quickly it would arrive. In fact, when I got home there was all sorts of talk flying around that the club were trying to sign a new central defender and I had that on my mind. Aberdeen's Willie Miller was being talked about as well as Craig Paterson of Hibs. I must admit that I wondered a little if all my efforts in Spain would count for nothing – and remember the games I had there came after just over twenty first-team games with Rangers. That's all I could manage because of my terrible injury run.

But I was determined that nothing would stop me and so I got back into training and waited for any challenges which might emerge. In the end the club signed Craig Paterson, I was asked to play alongside him at the heart of the defence, and I was also asked to be captain of the team. Ally Dawson had been skipper but he was out through injury at the start of last year and he had also indicated that he didn't enjoy the role too much. He seemed to think that it affected his game because he had that extra on-field responsibility.

That is the way captaincy affects some players. At first the Boss told me that he would wait to see how I reacted, that maybe he would try someone else. Perhaps he felt that I would be like Ally and tense up but that's not my way. I really enjoy being captain.

And what a start we had to the season, a run of over twenty games without defeat, but also games where we were playing really good football. Everything looked set for the kind of season we all wanted so much for ourselves and for the fans. Then, after the Cologne game it all fell apart. It's still hard for some of us to take it in. I think they had six shots at goals that night in Cologne and they scored with five of them. It was one of those nights when you felt that any time they tried a pot for goal they would probably score. That followed on top of a defeat from Celtic at Parkhead and suddenly we were a nervous team and points were lost. Injuries arrived, too, and while I kept clear of them Craig Paterson eventually suffered the same kind of debut season as I had had. It was almost as if there was a jinx operating on any new central defenders that the club bought. The result was that we found our partnership broken up and the back four from then on was being constantly rearranged. Like I said before, you work hard to get an understanding and then injuries destroy it. That goes some way towards explaining what happened to us.

But you cannot afford to have too many slips in the Premier League. It is an amazingly competitive league to play in. I didn't know too much about the domestic game in Scotland until I joined Rangers. You get the odd clip on the telly down south but usually that's only the big games. Perhaps an Old Firm match or a Cup final or something like that. Playing in the games has shown me just how hard it is. Friends of mine have come over from Northern Ireland to watch me play and they have all been surprised at the pace of the games. A whole lot of them quite often go across to England to see First Division games there and, as well as that, they get a regular diet of English games on the box. But all of them have been quite insistent that the game in Scotland is much faster.

They also find it more entertaining. Teams, for the most part, are going out to try to win games and there are more goals, more goalmouth incidents, more of the kind of play that the supporters on the terracings like to see. There have been arguments about the size of the League again this year among the legislators. Some have wanted the size increased, others wanted it to stay the same. Well, as a player relatively new to the whole business I think that it is by far the best league which can be operated in Scotland for now.

It isn't ideal, I suppose, for teams to meet each other four times in every season, and with Cup games thrown in there is bound to be a certain repetition. But where else was there a league which went undecided to the last day of the season? In England Liverpool ran away with the title, but in the Scottish Top Ten there were three teams who could all have taken it on that last day. Dundee United were the team who succeeded, Celtic finished second and the European Cup Winners' Cup holders Aberdeen were third. What that meant was as thrilling a final day as you could get anywhere. It also meant three full houses at the grounds where the games were played. Dundee United's game against Dundee at Dens Park saw the gates closed . . . it was the same at Pittodrie where Aberdeen played Hibs and it was very close to the 44,000 capacity at Ibrox where we met Celtic. That is a very healthy sign . . . and no one has to tell me that it would be even healthier still if Rangers had been involved in that last day finale. We weren't, of course, but we intend to be involved next year. That is something that we want desperately.

It will be a good competitive Premier League next season, too. The two newly promoted teams will help swell the attendances. Hearts' support speaks for itself . . . when we played against them in the League Cup semi-finals we had around forty-thousand fans at the two games. That's when they were still in the First Division remember! St Johnstone, too, can attract a reasonable support and they will be involved in quite a few local 'derbies' with the two Dundee clubs on their doorsteps.

With Aberdeen's success in Europe, and the two new teams, I believe that a revival from ourselves would give the game a magnificent boost in Scotland. The quality is there, the people

McClelland in action – a sight Rangers fans eventually welcomed last season!

are coming back through the turnstiles and we have to do our best to make sure that they are flooding back to Ibrox as well as going to the other grounds.

As I've said, it is hard to play in the Premier League. Defenders don't get too much time to dwell on the ball. I keep pointing that out to Dave McPherson on the park, trying to guide him a little. Dave has so much ability that he is still inclined to take a chance or two in the penalty box. In the Premier League that can be a killer. In Europe you can do it . . . in Scotland it's better most of the time not to try!

That's how hard it is. There are a few very good players too but don't expect me to name them. I never do that. I don't like letting on to an opponent that there are times he can give me trouble. In my view all I would be doing is giving them an edge the next time we play. But I know the good players and I think I know how to cope with them.

I'm still just twenty-seven years old but suddenly I'm the veteran of a Rangers team which has changed dramatically. One year I was a newcomer lacking in experience, the next I was one of the most experienced lads around. That's why I think that we can be a better team, a more consistent team this season. The younger players have had a chance to bed down, to get used to each other. And while I finished the season playing at left back, I felt more comfortable there than I did in that nightmare start with the club. That's because familiarity has brought more confidence to my game. It will do the same for the others. No one in the League played better than we did when we kicked off last season. The target this time has to be to start that way and to keep it going until the death. Let's hope that there will be a four-club battle for the title and that we can take it.

Oh, and let's hope that I can help the team win a Cup. Nothing would give me greater pleasure than lifting a trophy high above my head at Hampden.

It would give me great personal pleasure because I would feel that I'd proved a point – that a player from the Fourth Division can succeed. Then it would be nice to think that the guy who phoned in to Radio Clyde after that Old Firm game would have the guts to phone in once more, this time to apologize!

But, that's a selfish little thing. More than anything I'd like to hold that Cup up to the fans at the Rangers end. The same ones I suppose they would be who remained behind to cheer us after we had lost to Aberdeen in extra time last season. They showed us then that they still believed in us. We have to give them something tangible back in return for that belief. I'd like to be the captain to do that.